Restore the Heart | Restore the Home

Redesign

Angela Block

Ruth Many Blessings! ♡ Angela

Designer secrets to restoring your heart and your
home from the chaos of everyday life.

Table of Contents

DEDICATION

RYAN, I AM SO THANKFUL FOR THE FAMILY WE HAVE FOUGHT TO RAISE *together. I love you for putting up with my forever changing décor and crazy design ideas. Thank you for believing in me to write and publish this book, and for gracefully taking care of our family while I wrote it, sprained ankle and all.*

Kids, you are a piece of my heart. It has been a joy and a stretch to raise you. You have taught me so much about living out the grace of Jesus. Live your lives to your fullest potential in Jesus. I know you will do great things in Him. I am so thankful and proud of each of you.

Grandma and Grandpa, you passed away while I was writing this book. Your imprint on my life has been a pivotal one, showing me what it means to have a cozy home with arms wide open. You left us a legacy of faith, and I pray I can carry this legacy on for my children, and their children one day.

Thank you to my fabulous clients for giving me the opportunity to work with you. You taught me so much about design as we worked together. You have helped inspire this book.

Thank you to my talented interior design teachers. Also, to my amazing friends for believing in me when I couldn't, and for mentoring me in my faith journey. I have grown so much through your encouragement in my life.

My wonderful parents-in-law: thank you for your support, and for how you have taught us to run a home and our wonderful business. I so appreciate your faith and love for our family.

Mom and Dad, you taught us how to open our door to those who need a friend and a good meal. Thank you for laying a solid foundation of faith and showing us what it means to fight for our family. Thank you for always supporting my design endeavours.

Lord, I am amazed by your unconditional love and the grace you have for us. How you desire to bring us to a place of freedom by using ordinary people to share their stories to heal someone else's pain. Thank you for leading and writing this book. I cannot take credit for the words on these pages. Every piece of this book has been written only by your grace, mercy, and timing as you worked in my life. Your message was to be shared with the world, and I pray it be used for your glory to restore many hearts and homes.

Introduction

WELCOME HOME, MY BEAUTIFUL FRIEND! HOW DO YOU FEEL WHEN you think about your home? Do you feel joyful? Peaceful? Are you excited to come home at the end of the day? Or do you feel stressed and anxious, dreading the moment you walk in the door? Unfortunately, home may not always be a place you enjoy because of hurts and frustrations you experience there. Sometimes, it can actually be where the most chaos happens in our lives! Right? Let's find freedom for your home together, my friend!

I totally get the exasperation of trying to decorate your home around a busy family. You know, like when your kids throw your new designer pillows all over the floor just to step all over them, or they make your living room into one giant fort? Or when it feels like no one can get along in the house and you're ready to throw in the towel … (Can you adopt a new family? Is there such a thing?)

With home being where my heart lies, my early mommy years were spent desperately trying to decorate my home all pretty. But not knowing how, I would spend my precious budgeted birthday money on new décor that did absolutely nothing to enhance my space! Have you experienced this? Decorating books would give me one or two ideas with some design inspiration (which can be fun), but they still didn't tell me how to redesign my home. In my frustration, I decided to take interior design courses, which took me thousands of dollars and years to learn. Little did I know it would turn into the career of my dreams!

Being certified in interior design, staging/redesign, and colour consulting, I have worked with many wonderful homeowners. Some of which were in broken places because of various life circumstances. I have had many adventures working alongside my husband, Ryan, and his family, for our home building and renovation company. Ryan and I have also built a few of our own homes while raising our three kids together. All this has inspired my heart to empower you to find freedom for your home with the simple designer steps I personally use on every home I redesign.

"Wow, this is absolutely fabulous! I have never known how to arrange my furniture. I love my home now! Maybe I won't even sell it." I will never forget the moment an excited homeowner walked into her newly redesigned home. Our staging class had spent the afternoon rearranging her furniture, adding in a few new accessories to make it selling ready.

This is the power of interior redesign, my friend. Many homeowners are waiting until they have the money to do an expensive update, or even move to create the home they always hoped for. But interior design doesn't have to be complicated or costly. Updating a few accessories, rearranging your existing furniture, and maybe even adding a fresh coat of paint to the walls, may just be all it takes to create a space you love! Together we will learn how to create an inspiration board, layout your room, rearrange your furniture and accessories, and even shop for a few new pieces, all within your budget. Are you ready to bring your home to the next level in redesign?

Your life may not look as you envisioned with the white picket fence and perfectly clean children playing sweetly in the yard. Stresses and distractions may be taking you further and further away from pivotal family time. Creating a functional, beautiful space where we have time to make silly memories together instead of living life in chaos, has become crucial for our families to fight to stay together. Your heart may need some redesigning as well to find the joy in everyday life.

My prayer for you as you read on, is that you find peace in your heart … and your home. To rest your head at the end of a busy day, create amazing memories with the ones you love, while reaching out to those in need around you.

How to use this book

This book, though all about redesigning your home, is much about restoring your heart at the same time, because that is where the peace begins. You may want to read this book like a novel: chapter by chapter, then apply the design steps in the last chapter. Or, leave the heart restoration as a separate read to inspire your heart while sipping on your morning coffee. Read through the design principles before applying the steps in the last chapter.

I would love for you to really use this book: carry it around with you, scribble, make notes, buy another copy for a friend. However you use it, my greatest desire is that you find peace and restoration in a new way as you apply these steps ... because when your heart is restored, your home is restored too!

Chapter
One

BREATHE

"He leads me beside peaceful streams."
—Psalms 23:2 NLT

IT'S TIME TO BREATHE, MY FRIEND. LIFE IS TOO STRESSFUL AND OVER-
whelming these days, isn't it? It is time to let go, and well, just breathe.

Your family needs you to breathe too. On the airplane, they say put your oxygen mask on first in an emergency, so you can take care of your family. Peace in your home starts with you finding peace. This is key for our families to stay healthy. Crazy, huh? It won't help anyone if you're constantly distracted, barely surviving. When we get overwhelmed, our work suffers, we suffer, and our family suffers.

When did our lives get so cluttered and busy? Somehow, our lives have gotten so crammed that time to play has been put on the back burner. Our jobs come with us to the bathroom, the bedroom, and the dinner table with constant access to messaging and social media. We have lost the art of rest, but rest is actually a pivotal piece to do our work more effectively. We are more successful and productive when we take breaks. Allow room to breathe so you can get inspired again. Life should be a balance of faith, work, play, and rest. It may be time to shift our schedules to make time to find the joy in everyday life again.

So just breathe now. Breathe in the goodness of the Lord, and all He has blessed you with. Spend time in worship to reflect. Feels impossible with the long list of stuff you must get done, doesn't it? I know, I get it! I am a volunteering, working, taking care of the home and kids' kind of mom, let alone making space to breathe or laugh with my family. Are you kidding me?

"Ange, go turn on a dance song and shake it off in your living room with your kids." A dear friend told me this one day while I was losing my marbles, drowning in stress and chaos. Realizing that my busy, stressed out, mama heart was affecting my husband, family, and friends, I needed to make room to breathe and not take everything so seriously. Since then, due to life's sweet and painful interruptions, I have slowly been taking things off my list to make room for what is important at this stage of life. I realized that being a mom and wife was more important than sticking my hands in so many pots (we all need reminders). Taking a few things off my plate helped me be more effective in where I put my time. Room on the calendar was the ticket to allowing space for rest and life unexpected without getting my panties all tied up in a knot. You know?

Our families will thrive if we take life a little less seriously, look past our phones once in a while, and rest with our family. I mean, really spend time with them. Not with that blank look while the to-do list is running through our heads, but really pour into them. Your family will settle down when you do. Refocusing will give you the desire to enjoy your spouse (Yup, they need you, and you need them too!), with time to be silly together without the honey do lists.

They love you just as you are, so just be beautiful you. Breathe so you can breathe life into others. Believe me, I am still working through this one myself, but what a difference it has made to enjoy life again, and see joy happen in my family's hearts too! Taking time to breathe will help you be more effective in your work, your marriage will thrive, and your children will be more peaceful (or at least seem less annoying). They will learn how to live life in healthy balance, and you will have time to be an encouragement to others. It doesn't do anyone any good if you are falling apart!

Creating time to breathe will help you enjoy those you love without missing those special little moments. If you can't beat them, join them in the silly. Make work fun by getting your family involved in the process. It's good for them to learn to help! Our kid's behaviour can even shift when we become thankful and make time to enjoy everyday life!

Breathe, my friend, and put on your oxygen mask so you can thrive. Remember you are not a super woman. We have a Saviour who already saved the world, so you don't have to.

A friend once said to me that life is like juggling. We will never be able to perfectly balance all the balls, especially if we have too many balls all up in the air at one time. Remember we have seasons in our lives and this too shall pass. It's important to focus your priorities for this stage of life, giving you the ability to evaluate what to say yes to and when to say no, so you are doing what you need to do well.

How can you breathe? Take breaks, put aside your phone, go for an evening out with friends, or go for a walk. And at the very least, rest your head at the end of the day giving your plans over to our beautiful Saviour. He waits for us to lean on Him for strength and guidance daily. Being in worship and thanksgiving can really break the cloud of anxiety. You can't do it all, my beautiful friend. Let go and trust the Lord to lead you. Put your focus on Him first to bring balance and live life with intention.

A simple prayer

I cannot, Lord, but you can. I need you to lead me today, Jesus and bring it all together for your glory. Help me to live a life of victory and intention. Help me to enjoy this day because this is the day that you have made. Help me to know what to say yes to, what to let go of, and most of all, may my heart be in worship for you as I live out my days. I pray I can sit at your feet and rest in your loving presence. Help me to refocus and breathe. May your love spill into all that I do and all who I encounter. In Jesus' name, amen.

HOME IS WHERE THE HEART IS

A common saying is "Home is where the heart is". A definition for this may be: home is where you feel the most love. It needs to be a place of safety, refuge, and rest at the end of your stressful day. Where beautiful memories are created, perfection is not demanded, but cozy spaces are.

When I think of a home full of love, I think of my grandparent's home. There was always soft worship music playing in the background with a huge hug waiting for me as I walked in the door. Coffees, amazing food, and sweet conversations were surrounded by vibrant smelling flowers, hand-picked from the garden. Grandma was busy caring for her home, but she always had time to play a board game or bake with us.

What reminds you of a home full of love? How can you create a place where you can rest your head and find peace at the end of your day?

So, what if your home feels stressful? People often call me to redesign their spaces after a big life change due to moving, illness, divorce, or even the passing of a loved one. They want to create a space they can call home after their world has just been shaken. I get this! When we have just moved (which we do quite often), I don't feel like I can focus very well on anything else until my home is in order. My family always takes a while to settle in and adjust again too. How do you feel when your home life is in chaos? How can you even be successful in your everyday life? Imagine how your spouse, kids, or grandkids feel?

Women thrive on forming a cozy, inviting nest for their family and friends to enjoy, while men desire to build a safe and financially secure home. To create a "safe nest", it is important to take care of your home, so you have a safe place to bring your family together, away from this broken world.

At a women's conference I went to years back, we were asked, "What brings you peace?"

One woman's response was "When my kitchen counters are clean." We all laughed and totally agreed! Isn't that so true? Somehow, when the kitchen counters are clean, the rest of the house feels in order (sort of). Likewise, when our homes and families are somewhat organized, we feel settled and ready for the day ahead.

Here are some simple ways to create a peaceful home:

Organizing your home life

» Set some life goals. Establish a new balanced schedule with time for accomplishing lists, rest, work, and play time.

» Have a dance party in the kitchen while cooking, cleaning, or baking together. This can build some seriously fun and silly memories.

» Eat dinner together.

» Have a short daily clean up routine to keep your home tidy.

» Declutter your stuff regularly. This also keeps your house clean and lifts a huge weight of stress. Stuff can tend to create a huge burden on us. The less you own, the freer you may feel. Keeping your home decluttered may be super helpful in creating a cozy home your heart can thrive in. Remove anything that you don't love, does not have a purpose, or is not used regularly. Always have a box ready to go to the second-hand store and throw out your garbage.

» Get creative with your storage so everything you own has a home; this helps keep your home clutter free. Use furniture that has plenty of room for storage. This could be end tables with drawers, a wall of cute shelves, a storage ottoman, or a small dresser where your television sits. Even a hutch or buffet can be a great option to hide things away. When you have a space to put everything away, your home is easier to tidy up. Bonus … you will be able to find things when you need them!

Here is a fun vignette that includes some great storage for the kitchen

Spending money on your home

Are you struggling to justify spending time or money on your home to make it cozier? I understand spending money on your home can feel selfish and unimportant when there are so many other things we could spend our money on, as we are called to be good stewards with our money.

» Did you know that when we are faithful with little, we are blessed with more? Being a good steward is about sharing what we have been blessed with, including opening our homes to those around us.

I feel like the Lord wants to bless you with a beautiful home you can enjoy and share with others! He created all things beautiful. Just look around at nature. He loves beauty! He created you beautiful in His image. Why not make your home a beautiful place you can enjoy? It doesn't have to cost a lot to restore your home to its full potential. Simply rearranging your existing furniture and accessories will help enhance the beauty of your home. Sometimes this is all we need to love our home again.

» Owning a home with good resale value can actually be a good financial return. Make good investments in your home. Before you spend money on your home, ask yourself, "Have I shared a small portion of my budget with those in need?". Will this give me a good return on my investment? Will this enhance my life somehow? Is this within my budget?

Freshen up your home on a tight budget

» The thrift store can be quite a fabulous way to find a few treasures on a tight budget. Restore your treasures by painting an old picture frame or a fun piece of furniture. Dress up some vintage books by pulling off the covers and tying them together with a ribbon.

» Purchasing new table lamps, accent pillows, a throw, and maybe even a new piece of art at your favourite décor store, will go a long way on a tight budget to freshen up your redesign.

» Recover old accent pillows using fabric remnants that suit your accent colours.

» Paint your walls or existing furniture with a fresh coat of paint. Paint can be one of the least expensive ways to transform a space.

This second-hand bench was purchased for the entryway. A fresh coat of paint blends it perfectly into the décor.

» Try pieces from another room in your home in your redesign.

» Include your kids. Get your kids to paint a picture on large canvas for your living room wall using your accent colours (think of how excited they will feel to see their art up on the wall). Hang a ribbon like a banner across an empty wall to hang their most recent art pieces using clothespins. Get creative with canning jars.

» Hang a gallery of family photos and special pieces on one designated wall in your living room or hallway. Your family will appreciate seeing themselves on the wall and show visitors who you are.

Decorating with pets in your home

Decorating around pets can feel daunting, but there are some cute ways to incorporate them into your redesign without feeling like they have taken over. Building their needs into your existing décor, will help keep your space looking clean and clutter free. Just like with our kids or grandkids, we need to have spaces for their toys to tuck away at the end of the day. Your pets are a part of the family after all.

» Have a fabric dog bed that matches your accent colours. Change it up regularly to keep it looking fresh.

» Make room in the bottom of your kitchen cabinets or under a console table for the dog dishes or crate to tuck under.

» Have a special basket that suits your décor for their toys and grooming care.

We incorporated this bird cage into the design of this bird lover's home.

Creating a faith-filled home

Creating a faith-filled home is important. We need to put Jesus first in our lives, this is how we find balance to do everyday life. By living a faith-based life, we find our homes become cozier and more peaceful, filled with His love and grace for one another.

> *Fix these words of mine in your hearts and minds; tie them as symbols on your hands and bind them on your foreheads. Teach them to your children, talking about them when you sit at home and when you walk along the road, when you lie down and when you get up. Write them on the doorframes of your houses and on your gates, so that your days and the days of your children may be many in the land the Lord swore to give your ancestors, as many as the days that the heavens are above the earth. If you carefully observe all these commands I am giving you to follow – to love the Lord your God, to walk in obedience to him and to hold fast to him – then the Lord will drive out all these nations before you, and you will dispossess nations larger and stronger than you.*
> —Deuteronomy 11:18–23 NIV

» Hang artwork with scripture or write an inspiring verse on a chalkboard as an anchor for your day.

» Build a cozy corner somewhere in your home (almost like a prayer closet) where you can spend some quiet time with Jesus every day to journal, pray, read scripture, or just to sit to restore your soul.

» Pray through your home often and for everyone who lives there. Prayer is a powerful weapon to change the atmosphere and invite the peace of the Lord into your home. Anoint your home with oil inviting the Lord to cleanse and fill it with His restoring presence. Pray that anything that needs to be removed would be removed. Pray your home would be a place of peace, rest, joy, and unity for your family, and for all those who come to visit.

» Whether you believe there is a spiritual enemy or not, the Bible talks about the footholds that can wreak havoc in our lives. Pray about what should be removed. You may be surprised but anything pertaining to witchcraft, fortune telling, and statues can open a doorway to chaos in our homes. It will be worth letting these things go, and you may see a freedom come into your home as you do this.

Don't try to create a perfect home, my beautiful friend. This doesn't exist. The need for perfection can take away from the joy of just being together, but freedom to live in grace and mercy brings much joy. Create a cozy home where relationships are built so you can thrive in your everyday life. We are all shaken at times when hardship comes our way and that's okay, because if your foundation lays in the One who created you, you will find freedom again even if your heart or home falls apart for a moment. Let's get started in the restoration process…

Chapter
Two

FOCUS

> *"Come," he said. Then Peter got down out of the boat, walked on the water and came toward Jesus. But when he saw the wind, he was afraid and, beginning to sink, cried out, "Lord, save me!" Immediately Jesus reached out his hand and caught him...*
> —Matt 14:29–31 NIV

WHERE ARE YOU HEADED, MY FRIEND? DO YOU HAVE A VISION FOR YOUR life? Or are you going through the motions following wherever life takes you? It can feel a little uneasy when we lack direction, can't it?

Knowing where we are headed helps keep us away from distractions and fear that pull us around when life storms come our way. This helps us to live life on purpose and not waste our short time here on earth.

What we see in front of us is where we tend to follow, where we follow can shift our perception. Not having focus in your life can be a scary place to be, especially if what is going on in your life is unsettling. The Bible tells us, *"So we don't look at the troubles we can see now; rather, we fix our gaze on things that cannot be seen. For the things we see now will soon be gone, but the things we cannot see will last forever."* 2 Cor 4:18 NLT.

Like Paul when he walked on the water with Jesus in the above scripture, he was able to stay steady when his eyes were fixed on Jesus, but quickly started to drown when he looked around him in fear.

So where is your focus right now, dear friend? Do you look to media or people for direction? Are you listening to the world's standards? Do you feel inspired as you do? Or does it leave you feeling discouraged and discontent, desperately trying to measure up to this world's version of perfect? The illusion of perfect can be such a distraction in our lives. I don't know about you, but I feel like I am drowning just trying to keep up to the lies, pressure, and unrealistic expectations of this ever-changing world around us.

What if perfect was never the goal? Trying to achieve perfection (which is unattainable in this broken world), we actually miss out on the beauty of the journey we are in, and all we have been blessed with. We can quickly forget where we were headed in the first place!

I so get it! I spent many years agonizing over trying to be good enough as I put my focus on the world around me. This only created discouragement, constantly comparing myself to the skinnier person, or the perfect home I see in the media. I worked hard trying to measure up and impress people, only to feel even more insecure after. I would get so frustrated when my family didn't fit into my idea of perfection. My unrealistic expectations created a lot of stress and anxiety in our home, leaving me to crumble when things got tough and the storms of life came.

When I realized that the world's standards were not realistic, and that my focus needed to be on Jesus and what His word says for my life, I slowly learned to embrace the beauty of the journey with all of it's imperfections, knowing that this is what makes me and my story unique. This is where I found freedom to just be who I was created to be.

Spending time with Jesus in prayer daily, reading His word, and creating goals gives me fresh vision to live freely, focused and on purpose.

His word creates a measuring stick for everything we do. This gives us the freedom to let go of the things that don't fit within our goals (within reason of course), while still making room for the God interruptions … they are always worth it.

How to refocus your vision

» Set aside some time to pray and reflect on the word of God daily. What do you feel when you do?

_____

» Set some goals for your life.

» Monthly

_____

_____

» Yearly

_____

_____

» 5 years from now

_____

_____

» Your life goals

_____

_____

» Where do you spend most of your time currently?

_____

_____

» What changes do you need to make to achieve your goals and stay focused on what is important?

_____

_____

» Are these changes healthy long term? Do they line up with scripture? Or are they a temporary "make me happy" change?

_____

_____

» Make a list of what you need to do to accomplish these goals.

_____

_____

_____

» Pin your list up somewhere where you will see it to help you stay focused.

> *"For the word of God is alive and active. Sharper than any double-edged sword …"* —Hebrews 4:12 NIV

You can do this, my friend! You can live a life of freedom and purpose when you put your focus on the truth, rather than getting pulled into the lies of the temporary world around us. We cannot do this life alone, friend. We need Godly people in our lives to help us stay focused and get inspired. Learn to ask for help!

The Lord's plans for you are good and will prevail when you trust and follow Him for your tomorrows … even when the storm rages around you.

Prayer

Lord, give me strength to stay firm in your truth to live a life of purpose and intention. Thank you for your direction in my life and that you have a good future in mind for me. I don't need to fear what I am going through because you have good plans for me and my family. I give my plans over to you to be aligned in your direction for my life. I pray for Godly people who can inspire my walk to go deeper and keep me joyful and focused as I walk the good walk of faith in your word, in Jesus' name, amen.

INSPIRATION

Let's finally dive into the redesign process. Are you ready? Me too! I am absolutely excited to show you some tools to redesigning your own home.

Interior design is all about creating a cohesive, functional space by using what you love and making it beautiful. Your space should be a reflection of who you are.

Redesign is an extension of interior design by incorporating what you own, rearranging it to be more functional, while enhancing the features of your home. Almost like an invitation to come on in and enjoy the space the way it was intended to be enjoyed.

Let's start by getting inspired, because that's where we find direction for your redesign ...

Move ahead with this in mind:

- » Keep what adds to your space and tells your story.
- » Let go of anything that takes away from the feel of the vision
- » Incorporate a few pieces you love, but don't hold on too tightly to anything that doesn't work. You have permission to get rid of it, sell it, or give it to someone in need.
- » Don't be afraid to get creative and break a few rules occasionally. Interior design is art after all.

Lesson One: How to get inspired

You may wonder how to even begin. I have moments like this too. Getting creative requires time to breathe, allowing your mind to rest. It helps to relax with a cup of tea or coffee while looking through home décor pictures to get inspired. Social media or magazines can be a great place to stir your inner creative side. You do have a creative side deep down in there somewhere, my beautiful friend …

Inspiring photos help give you direction for your redesign.

Bookmark inspiring images that appeal to you, then narrow them down to a couple of favourites. What about each picture is speaking to you? Carefully look at the details in these photos. What is the common theme running through these images? Is there a more traditional feel about them? Do they all have bright colours? Is the flooring similar in each picture? Make notes of the common themes that draw you to these photos. (There will be room to write down your answers later, so feel free to read on at this point.) The images that inspire you may all be quite different, but by pulling out the common themes that attracted you to these photos will give you a clearer vision on how to personalize your redesign.

Lesson Two: Style in interior design

There are so many fabulous styles out there. We all have different tastes that appeal to us. This is what makes you unique. So, feel free to create your own flavours in your space. Understanding the style of your home, your needs, likes and dislikes will help pull together your vision for your new space more effectively, leaving your space feeling cohesive and balanced as you get creative.

I had a client show me a contemporary glass dining table she was thinking of purchasing for her new space. She had previously requested a more traditional look for her room, so I asked her if this was really what she wanted. She admitted that as attractive as these modern tables were, she preferred a warmer more traditional wooden table. Either option would have worked great in her space, but knowing her style, we were able to move forward with the vision she preferred rather than ending up with a design she didn't love.

Different styles in interior design

Traditional

» Calm, classic, and elegant using cozy, detailed, luxurious fabrics. Furniture with curvy detailed lines on deep rich dark wood tones.

Modern

» Simple, airy feeling furniture with lots of clean straight lines and some natural elements. This modern style has a mid-century feel. No fuss, no muss equals a simple sophisticated space.

Contemporary

» A modern style combined with the current trend. Clean lined furniture helps define this style.

Eclectic

»   A combination of a few different styles all incorporated together. This is tricky to get
right without looking messy, but done right, it can be a fun unconventional space.

Scandinavian

» Modern, clean, simple, fresh and airy, with functional minimalistic styled furniture. Incorporates bright colours easily, but lends itself nicely to a natural feeling space as well.

Country, cottage or farmhouse

» Cozy, vintage, worn or lived in feeling, with lots of natural textures such as baskets, natural rugs and linens, painted wood, soft curvy lined furniture, powdery colours, garden flowers, shiplap or bead board panelled walls. Can be a mix of contemporary and traditional lines.

Industrial

» A warehouse rustic feel, with contemporary natural elements, heavy industrial metals, and natural woods.

Coastal

»   Breezy, light and airy, fresh natural wood tones, contemporary furniture, and striped fabrics. Think beach house or sandy beaches.

As you can see, there are so many fabulous styles out there. This is only a few of the basic styles to available. Are you wondering if you can mix any of these together? My advice is absolutely! But try not to mix more than two styles together or you could end up with a bit of chaos … which will defeat the purpose of creating a peaceful feeling home.

Maybe your home has a modern feel, but you prefer a more country feel? Or you love a contemporary design with a few traditional elements (such as a transitional style). Using the existing style of your home, add in the elements of the style you want to incorporate, and repeat both styles relatively equally throughout the space to tie them together. Stay consistent using these styles throughout the rest of your home to keep everything flowing sweetly from room to room.

Modern farmhouse-styled kitchen

Changing your current style

This book is all about refreshing your space by using what you have. But what if you currently have a style in your home you are well, just tired of? Here are a few cost-effective things you can do to update that style: sell some of your old accessories and furniture to put the money towards new accessories. Paint your walls and some of your old furniture to suit the fresh new style.

If you have a larger budget to work with, update a few of your fixed elements: such as paint your kitchen cabinets, change the kitchen backsplash and countertops, update the flooring, put on new trim and baseboards, or change up your fireplace surround. Some new furniture and accessories can help as well. Freshening up a few of these elements can make a big difference towards a getting a whole new style incorporated into your home.

Lesson Three: Creating an inspiration board

Do you ever go shopping and purchase new décor but when you bring it home, it doesn't enhance your space the way you had hoped? Now you have just spent your precious money, and you either need to keep it or return it, but you're still not sure how to achieve the look you are after. I know! I get it! I used to do this before I was trained too, so don't feel discouraged, my friend. This is what the inspiration board helps you with, knowing exactly which pieces to look for and why.

I used to walk through my favourite decorating stores and purchase my favourite pretty accent pillows or art piece only to get it home and find out it didn't suit at all. I think this is one of the biggest mistakes we tend to make; when we walk through a décor store, purchase our favorite pieces just because we like them, but the new pieces don't fit the vision, leaving us with a space that is not at all what we had dreamed of.

Shopping like this is like trying to fit five different puzzles together into one. None of the pieces will fit together very well, and it will end up being a confusing picture in the end. We need to choose items that bring the big picture together. By spending some time playing around to see what fits with each other in the space, you can shop with confidence knowing exactly what pieces are needed to bring the vision together.

An inspiration board puts all your ideas in one place to give you a clearer vision to move forward with for your interior redesign. This is a great way to see if your elements work well together, what should be removed, adjusted, or added to create a cohesive space before actually changing anything. Let's learn how to create your inspiration board.

Find your inspiration

» **Inspirational piece**

Decide on your needs, likes, and dislikes for your redesign. Choose your favorite inspirational piece to build your vision around. This could be an antique dresser, a piece of art with colours you love, or an area rug you're not ready to part with. Sometimes it is a fixed element such as a fireplace or kitchen cabinets that may inspire your redesign.

The headboard became the inspiration for our redesign

» **Set the vision**

Looking through pictures, find inspirational images and a style you love that would suit your new space.

» **Create a floor layout**

Planning your layout helps to know what furniture pieces are needed, and what existing pieces will fit in the redesign. We will talk more about this in the next chapter.

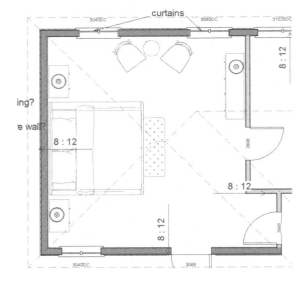

The furniture layout

Create your inspiration board

You can make your inspiration board by printing off pictures from online design stores or cutting them out of magazines to glue onto a white piece of paper. Don't glue until your vision comes together or you may end up with a messy paper! You could even try copying and pasting photos from online onto a slide document page to create your inspiration board. Make sure your background is white to get a true reading how of your pieces all work together. Sometimes I will apply the wall colour to my background as well, so I know how all the elements fit with my chosen paint colour.

The inspiration board

» **Start with your inspirational piece, furniture and fixed elements**

Starting with your inspirational piece, apply pictures of each piece of furniture you would like to incorporate into your board. Adding pictures of the existing or updated elements such as the kitchen, fireplace and flooring will also help anchor the feel for the space.

» Choose the wall colour

If the existing wall colour doesn't quite work in the new design, play around with other wall colours until all the elements pull together well.

» Accessories

This is the fun part! Play around with existing and new accessories until it feels peaceful to help you know what to shop for and what just won't work.

» Assess

Remember, this is about loving the big picture, not just about loving each piece, because if you use every piece you love, you may not end up loving the big picture in the end.

I will keep adding and taking away from the board until it feels like it sings to me. As you begin your own board, don't get discouraged; it may take some time until your eyes are trained to know what works well together and what doesn't. The more you do this, the better you will get! Better to play and make mistakes here than to spend a bunch of money on new furniture, or renovations only to find out it still doesn't really pull together.

This is where you may find out if the sofa needs an update, or your coffee table or fireplace brick may need to be painted. That's okay! These projects can be left for another day when you are ready, but at least you have a plan to move forward with one step at a time. Don't get overwhelmed with what you feel like you need to purchase. Think outside of the box to find a cost-effective solution if you don't have a large budget to work with. Can you paint it? Recover it? Use a piece from another room in your home? Purchase a second-hand item and paint it? If something still doesn't look right on your board, keep adding and taking away until it does feel right. Maybe adjust the colours making them lighter or darker or even use a different colour altogether if something doesn't feel right.

» Make a list

When the board feels complete, make a list of what projects need to be done, what needs to be removed from the room and what needs to be purchased based on the given budget. There is no need to tackle it all now; make a wish list to move forward with whenever you're ready.

MASTER BEDROOM LIST

Cozy Chair
end tables
accessories
bedding
throw
accent pillows
lamps
mirror
art
painting

Budget =

The shopping list

» **Shopping**

Inspiration board in hand, go shopping. I even pray about what to buy as I know the Lord is the one leading my hands and the vision. I may not know, but He does. I love that He cares for even these little things.

Take a picture of anything that speaks to you as you shop in stores or online, even if you end up with a dozen pictures of different area rugs. This will give you some great options to play around with on your inspiration board. You may not need to shop at all if it is not in your budget, but even setting aside a couple hundred dollars can get you a few new pieces such as lamps, art, and a few new throw pillows to help make your space feel brand new!

Shopping for accessories

This is a master bedroom I redesigned. We did nothing to change the fixed elements except for painting the walls and adding in some simple trim on the feature wall to give it some texture and elegance.

What was the inspiration for the room? The headboard, which was newly built by my clients' talented husband. We created the feel of the space around this urban elegance styled headboard, keeping in mind the style of the rest of her home. We purchased a few new accessories, end tables, and a chair. She painted her existing dressers to use what she already owned, which worked perfectly.

Before

After

Chapter
Three

DIVISION

> *"Love is patient, love is kind. It does not envy, it does not boast, it is not proud. It does not dishonor others, it is not self-seeking, it is not easily angered, it keeps no record of wrongs. Love does not delight in evil but rejoices with the truth. It always protects, always trusts, always hopes, always perseveres."*
> —1 Corinthians 13: 4–7 NIV

HOW IS YOUR HOME LIFE DOING, MY FRIEND? IS IT A TOUGH PLACE TO BE with much arguing and complaining? Do you know there is a very real enemy who seeks to devour our families? Unfortunately, division in our families often starts in our marriage. When we stay angry, justified in our hurt and pain, we give the enemy a foothold to stake a claim in our homes. This can quickly cause our marriage to fall apart. When our marriage breaks, our family breaks, and the very core of our foundation becomes shaken. Our home falls apart.

If we spend all our time spilling out our hurts at each other instead of loving one another, we quickly respond in anger, feeling justified in our pain. It's exhausting to be in that state of mind all the time, isn't it? Always thinking how we can hurt each other in response to the pain our spouse or kids have caused us. This keeps us from living in the joy and freedom our Heavenly Father intended for us to live. Bible verse, Matt 12:25 NIV says; *"… a household divided against itself cannot stand"*. Our homes will simply not stand if we stay angry with one another feeling justified in the hurt we are experiencing.

When our family falls apart, our focus can shift into the distractions of the world to ease the pain we are in. Beautiful families are swept up every day in the lie that it will be better if I just get out of this destructive home. But the problem is our hurts will continue to follow us into the next relationship, and the next, until the inner pain in our hearts is dealt with. So be brave, dear friend, and find healing for your heart so you don't point your anger towards the ones you love most.

We have all experienced the pain of divorce in some way which can cause hurts for many years to follow. But wherever you are at or what you have gone through, don't despair; it's not too late! Nothing we have gone through is wasted. Through Christ's redeeming love, there is always hope to rebuild a healthy home. Our redeemer is good at restoring us from the pit of destruction and making beauty from the ashes. Amazing grace, isn't it?

I totally get the pain anger can cause. We were not in a healthy place when we got married, I was only 18 and barely knew who I was at the time. We had to learn (the painful way) how to forgive, lay down our unrealistic expectations of each other, and how to communicate in a healthier way while we grew up and raised our busy little family together. This has taken loads of tears, with incredible peaks and deep valleys. We have had to learn to be selfless, to create healthy boundaries, and respect one another. Prayer and Godly counsel have been helpful for us to find healing and forgiveness for one other, to love each other unconditionally, just as Christ has loved us unconditionally.

It has been so worth it to fight for our family. Love is a choice and is always worth it. So, it may be time to lay down your hurt and break down the protective walls you've built to come in grace, love, and forgiveness even when you feel the other one doesn't deserve it.

What would happen if you put all the time you've spent being angry into forgiving one another instead? To respond with love no matter how the other one responds. Can you imagine what the response would be? Love will always prevail, create a bridge, while breaking down the division in our homes.

I know it can feel super scary to forgive and love again (This does not mean being a doormat so please find Godly help if you're not in a safe environment), but it's better to go through the pain to find healing, than to live in an angry divided house with walls up and miss out on love in its full. It may take some hard work to find restoration, but anything worthwhile will require much work and attention. I feel like we have forgotten what it means to work hard for something that doesn't come easy.

When my kids were little, and they would start to respond with impatience or anger towards each other, I knew it was time for a heart check for me. Kids copy what they see. I knew it was time for me to work through my own hurts or stresses I was going through at the time. How we respond to each other matters. And the change needs to start with you.

So be brave, dear friend, to heal those broken places in your heart. Give yourself grace as it may take time. Your family may not know what to do with this new you, but it will catch on. You may even see a big change in how everyone responds to each other. You may feel more peace and most of all, a sense of unity may happen in your home. Let love be the example for the next generation you are raising, so they can thrive.

Prayer

Lord, help me to let go of any resentment I am feeling. Forgive me for holding onto it and help me to forgive those who have hurt me. Please bring healing to my heart and my home. In Jesus name, Amen.

FUNCTION

How functional is your home right now? Having a practical space becomes super important when life gets busy, doesn't it? If you are living in an unfunctional space, you know just how frustrating it can be by adding to your already stressful life. For this reason, function is top priority in creating a well-designed room. There is no point in decorating a room all lovely, only to find it doesn't work in your everyday life. I will show you how to plan your layout, so your home can function to its fullest potential.

We all need to simplify our lives as much as possible while raising our busy families. Knowing where to find things when you need them, having a place to put them, with ease of moving around (not tripping over furniture that always seems to be in your way) is super important. We need room to breathe for our minds to feel free enough to enjoy everyday life. So whatever sized home you live in; minimal amount of furniture scaled to the size of the room, while being functional for everyday living, with loads of easy storage to hide the clutter is top priority.

We lived in my in-law's beautiful basement for seven months while we built our home (they were so gracious in letting us stay there!). During this time, we squished everything we could into their large basement suite to save on storage costs. It drove this organized interior designer crazy. I made the most of it, but the rooms felt heavy and cluttered. This made me feel discouraged and stressed out while we lived there. The extra storage solutions helped save my sanity by having a place to put things away and stay organized, but if I could have removed some of the heavy furniture, I think I could have actually enjoyed the cozy space so much more.

Every piece should enhance the function, flow, and purpose in some way. How does your space function right now? What changes do you need to make to meet your everyday needs?

Lesson Four: Creating a focal point

We all need a place to focus our eyes as we walk into a room. Your focal point should be the focus for your feature wall, while drawing your eyes to enjoy the beautiful features of the space. This creates purpose and breathing room as we walk in to our room. Without a main focal point, our eyes can feel overwhelmed not knowing where to look first. Adjoining walls are decorated to support and bring balance to the rest of the room.

Let's create a focal point for your space. You may be wondering what your focal point is. Walk out and back in. What do you notice first as you walk in? If it's clutter, don't worry, we will work on clearing that away. But quite possibly it's a fireplace, a beautiful window, or maybe a large empty wall … whatever it is, let's build your focal point on this wall so it becomes the feature of the room.

» If you have a fireplace, adding a large enough art piece and a few accessories will help draw your eyes to this feature wall. If you don't love your fireplace, some trim work, new rock, or even just paint can help freshen it up. Layering the right accessories and art may be all it needs to feel fresh and updated.

Before

After

» If your focal point is a large window wall with a beautiful view, arrange your furniture to enhance the view. Keep your curtains light and airy so as not to distract your eyes from the view. Likewise, if your view is nothing special, a patterned and more dramatic curtain can distract from the bad view while adding some fun design to the room.

» If you don't have any great focal points in your space, which is quite normal, let's create one! Which is the first wall you see when you first walk into the room? You'll want to create your focal point on this wall if it makes sense to do so. If not, search for the next best wall to build your focal point on. A sofa with a large piece of art centred above it, a couple of end tables, and some table lamps can create a fabulous focal point for the space. A faux homemade fireplace or even an electric fireplace for the wall with art above can make a great focal point as well.

» In your bedroom you can create your focal point with art and/or a headboard above the bed and two lamps on end tables on either side.

» In an entry, this would be a side table or a bench with art or a mirror above it, inviting you into the home.

Make sure your artwork is large enough to create impact to draw your eye to the focal point, so it doesn't feel lost on the wall.

Before   After

This room has a great focal point, but I feel like we're missing it with the seating being pushed against the walls in this large open concept room. By arranging a more intimate seating area, my clients were able to engage better with their guests while drawing notice to the beautiful focal point of the space. This room feels more inviting and may even end up being used more often. We need to tell our eyes where to look to enjoy the beauty of the room.

Fun ways to enhance a feature wall

Your feature wall may be just fine after it's styled with some art and accessories, but sometimes it could use a little extra character to make it stand out. Here are a few ideas to play around with.

Paint

»   Paint an accent colour on your feature wall if it suits the space. Make sure it's a bold enough contrast to the rest of the walls, such as; a few shades darker of the same colour, or a complementary accent colour. Chalkboard paint, or a combination of your accent colours in a fun artistic design can also be an inexpensive way to enhance your feature wall.

Wallpaper

»   Find a wallpaper that complements your style and the other colours in the room. I often choose a wallpaper that blends with the existing wall colour. Or, you could choose the wallpaper first and pull out one of the colours in the wallpaper to paint the rest of the walls within the room.

Panelled walls

» Adding texture to the wall using shiplap, beadboard, or moldings is a less demanding way to create a feature wall. I prefer to blend it with the wall colour or paint it the trim colour. The style of panelling you choose depends on the style of your home.

Brick or Stone

» Adding an earthy texture and feel brick may be fun in an industrial, modern, or Manhattan styled home. Stone adds to a west coast, contemporary, or cottage feeling space. The styles of rock vary quite a bit, so choose your rock and the colour based on the style you have in your home. The cost of the product and installation may cause this to be a pricier option.

Wood

» Cozy and earthy, wood paneling can be a great option for your rustic or farmhouse feeling home.

Built-in shelving

» Feature walls can include built-in shelving or cabinets to create extra storage while giving the space interest and texture. This can be a great way to display a few of your favourite accessory pieces.

Art

»   Hang a combination of favorite smaller art or family portraits together to create a lovely gallery wall.

The feature wall options really are endless, so feel free to get creative here, making sure it relates to the rest of the space and the style of your home.

Secondary focal points

The other walls in your room may need attention as well to create balance within the space. Art and/or furniture will help create your secondary focal points for the rest of the room. This could be a large wall with your sofa and artwork above it for your living room, or a wall with your dresser with a mirror above in your bedroom, or the empty wall in your office that calls for a cozy chair and a side table. Keeping the same principles as above, create a centred focal point for that wall as well. Don't worry too much about taking the focus off the focal point as your focal point will always remain the star of the show.

This dresser and mirror combination creates a great secondary focal point, creating balance for the focal point on the opposite wall.

Open concept rooms

In an open concept room, treat each designated area as its own room with its own focal point. If your dining room, kitchen, and living room are all in one large space, your focal point for your dining room could be a buffet with a large mirror above it, a large window with pretty curtains, or some large art on the wall. Using an area rug for each section can be a clever way to define each area. Your living room's focal point could be the fireplace, while the kitchen cabinets are the focal point for the kitchen.

If you have an extra-large master bedroom, define the bed area and the sitting area as their own spaces with their own focal points. If the room is a normal size, one main feature wall is all it needs (but adding in a small sitting area may still be nice to make it feel cozy).

Before   After

This wall was connected to the dining and living room in this large open concept area. Large pieces of art above the dining table creates a great focal point for the dining room, while adding art and accessories above the fireplace helps draw your eye to the main focal point for the living room.

Lesson Five: Function and flow

Every piece in your space needs to have a purpose to function well. Knowing your needs helps you plan your pieces of furniture accordingly.

What are your needs for your space?

» **Exterior**

The front exterior of your home should reflect what's inside and who you are. This is people's first impression of you, so you want it to be somewhat good! Potted shrubs on either side of your front door with a fresh coat of paint on your trim, front door, and/ or siding can help with this.

» **The entryway**

Your entryway needs to be an inviting welcome into the rest of your home, with a memorable goodbye. It should introduce a little taste of who you are and what your home is about. You may need seating for putting your shoes on, with storage for coats, and maybe even backpacks if you don't have a mud room. A place for dropping your keys and your purse is helpful as well. What are your needs for your entryway?

» **The living room or family room**

Living and family rooms should be a place to get silly and play, cozy up with a good book or a movie, and enjoy conversations with family and friends. Keeping it peaceful with lots of seating for easy conversation and a place to put down your coffee cup is important.

What do you need your living room for? Space for your piano or guitar? A place to meet with clients? Relaxing with your family? The television? Office space? More storage? A sleeping area for overnight guests?

» **Dining rooms**

Special and silly memories are made here for your family to gather and have beautiful conversations. Your dining area may be a formal room used only occasionally, or may be part of your kitchen and used every day, with highchairs and all. It should be an inviting space where people are excited to gather together and chat … Okay, eating is important there too.

What are your needs for this space? How many does it need to seat? Do you have little people that make messes, and it needs to be washable? Or is it only for adults and you want an area rug and fabric chairs? Does it need to function as an office or craft space? Do you need room for your hutch?

» **The office**

Okay, super serious now right? After all, it is your work space. But it actually should be a place to get creative and get inspired to do your work well. Treat your work space like its own oasis, not just another messy room in the back of the house. Is it just for the desk? Or do you have a home-based business with a need for lots of storage? Do you need seating for clients? Or a place to hide away with a good book?

» **The bedroom**

Your bedroom should feel dreamy and romantic, like a secret hideaway. Stating the obvious here but your bedroom should be a place to rest. Your main focal point is usually the wall where you put your bed. Centre your bed on the large wall opposite from the door to the hallway. Add in a headboard or large pieces of art to create a focal point above it. End tables with chunky lamps on either side seem to anchor the wall. Minimize your dressers in the room and add in a cozy chair or two instead. If you have the space, hide your dressers or most of your clothing in the closet. I even have my makeup vanity in my walk-in closet to keep my room from feeling cluttered. What are your needs for your bedroom?

» **The rec room or playroom**

This is where things get super relaxed with a place to play and just hang out. What are your needs for this space? Do you need room for a home gym? A sitting area for sofas to relax on while watching movies and playing video games? Do you need storage for games and toys? Incorporate these into your room's design.

Make it functional

When you know the needs for your room, you need the right furniture to make it happen. Here are a few important questions to keep in mind when deciding on furniture for your room.

» **Will this function in our everyday living?**

Have you ever been at someone's house, and it feels so perfect you are afraid to sit down? Not very inviting is it? Pretty should never overtake our invitation for people to come and enjoy the space. Make function your top priority when designing your space.

I really wanted a creamy sofa, but I knew I would somehow find a way to dump coffee on it, or my kids would make it look dirty over time. To me, having a stained sofa would look worse than the darker fabric, so I chose the charcoal sofa option instead. I lightened the dark sofa by adding lighter accent pillows. If the sofa was going into a formal living room that would only be used occasionally for visiting or reading, I would have invested in the creamy coloured sofas instead.

The charcoal sofas were a more functional option in this neutral styled family room. Styling with lighter accessories helps lighten the dark sofas.

» Is it useful?

To have a glass table in a small living room we lived in a few years ago would have been so nice and airy. But a storage ottoman was way more functional for much needed storage in our small space. Choosing a lighter fabric ottoman to lighten the space while meeting our storage issue would have made a great compromise.

» Does it fit?

Plan your room layout to be sure what you bring home fits well in your space. If it is too large for the room, it will feel tight and cluttered, which creates a mental block from wanting to come in. This makes us feel more anxious and stressed out.

If you ever look at a home that is staged for selling, there is minimal furniture with pieces that are scaled to the size of the room. This gives you the illusion this home will fit your everyday needs, even if it is teeny tiny.

Measure your hallways, doorways, and furniture before purchasing. We bought a cozy, oversized sectional for our basement man cave years ago, only to find out it didn't fit through the doorways or stairwell! We fought with it for a while (okay, a long while) and finally managed to squeeze it in. When we moved out, we did manage to squeeze it out again (only by a complete miracle!) and move it into our next home.

Then, when we moved again… we found out it didn't fit in our new house at all! We had larger doorways this time, but the angle into our new man cave didn't allow the sofa to fit. We ended up having to sell it and purchase a new sofa that came in smaller pieces that would fit through our basement hallways! So, learn from my mistakes and measure everything before purchasing.

Sometimes it is just about the pretty. And sometimes it's about choosing the more functional sofa to keep your sanity.

Rules for good traffic flow

» Furniture should be arranged to invite us into the room and draw our eyes to the features of the space.

» Keep your walkways flowing freely to walk around easily. Don't block walkways with furniture.

» Choose smaller, lighter, more airy furniture in small spaces to give the illusion of more space.

» Use larger, heavier furniture in larger rooms so they don't feel like they are tiny and floating away in your larger space.

» Create conversational areas within your living room by grouping your seating together to create an intimate conversational area.

» Keep a minimum of 3–4 foot walkway space in high traffic areas for ease of walking around.

» Leave roughly a 2-foot walkway between the sofa and coffee table for room to walk around, while keeping the area intimate and functional.

» Always use pieces that enhance the space in some way. Remove any that cause clutter.

» Do not place furniture on a wall three feet or smaller. This just makes the space feel cluttered.

Creating balance with your furniture

» All the backs of seating should be relatively similar heights throughout the space.

» Accessories such as lamps placed beside beds or sofas should be similar heights to each other on both sides, or a light fixture on one side with a floral arrangement of similar height on the other side helps create balance.

» End tables don't need to be the same end tables on either side, but do need to be similar heights on both sides, with a similar height as the sofa's arm.

» A coffee table is needed in a living/family room to ground the space and not feel like its floating away …

» A variety of different chairs around the dining table is possible, but keep the backs of the chairs in similar height and style to tie them together.

» Divide your space into four equal sections to help you create balance within the room. If there is an area feeling a little empty, fill it with a vignette to keep it from feeling heavier on one side than the other, such as a console table and art above, or two side chairs for a reading corner. If it's a main walkway, sometimes art on the wall will be enough to balance the room.

The supporting walls in a room are just as important to creating balance within the space as the focal point.

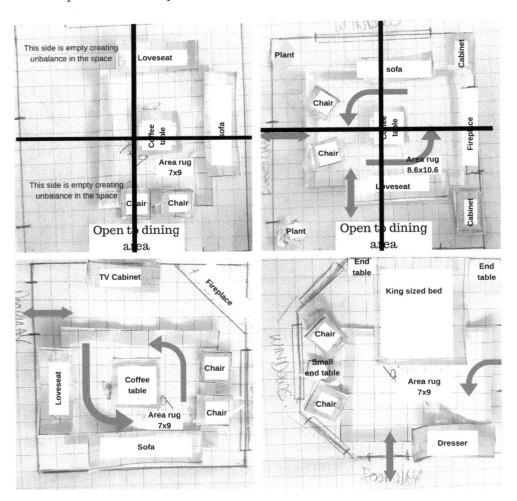

Lesson Six: Planning your layout

Create your furniture layout

Rearranging your furniture may feel daunting, but by measuring it out on paper, you can play around with it until the room feels balanced, flows well, and all the pieces have a purpose before doing any heavy lifting.

Start with rearranging the larger pieces of furniture such as your sofa, bed, or desk to enhance the focal point. Play around with these on paper to create a good flow of traffic. Then add in your accent furniture pieces such as your accent chairs, coffee table, end tables, dressers, or shelving to bring balance within the room.

Here is what you need to get started with your room layout. If you have an app or a design program, you are more than welcome to use those. I realize not everyone has access to these programs, so a good old-fashioned pencil and paper can go a long way to plan out your space. This format could be used to plan out your renovation as well … but that's for another time.

<u>Tools to plan your layout</u>
» Graph paper
» Pencil
» Measuring tape
» Ruler

<u>How do we create a room layout?</u>
1. Measure your space.
2. Draw out your room using one square = one square foot.
3. Draw in your fixed items scaled to their measurements such as your fireplace, window and doorways, and your kitchen if you have an open concept room.
4. Measure and cut out your furniture pieces on a separate piece of graph paper using one square = one square foot
5. Arrange your furniture in your paper room starting with your larger pieces, then add your accent pieces of furniture until it looks and feels just right.

Don't be afraid to get creative, but do confirm that everything feels balanced within the room. Function and flow need to be your focus… then comes the pretty. We will be rearranging your furniture for real a little bit later so let's read on, friend!

Chapter
Four

TRANSFORMATION

> *"Because your love is better than life, my lips will glorify you. I will praise you as long as I live, and in your name I will lift up my hands"*
> —Psalm 63:3-4 NIV

OH, DEAR FRIEND! YOU MAY BE GOING THROUGH THE DEEP OF THE deep in life. Where are you at right now? Do you feel hopeless with the situation you are facing? Are you battling past hurts, shame, condemnation, or regrets? Are you ready to push through the deep of the pain to find freedom? Or are you going to hide in self-destruction feeling justified in your hurt and fear?

We all experience pain in our lives that causes us to have to make some big changes. When the pain gets too difficult to handle, we finally break. This can be a sweet place to be, because we are forced to make some necessary decisions on how to move forward. It's what you choose in this broken moment that matters. It may be tempting to run from the pain you are experiencing right now, but I encourage you to persevere, my friend, because breakthrough is waiting for you. Don't give up now! Be brave to face the circumstances head on even though it may be painful to go through.

One of my biggest moments was when my second baby was born. She cried a lot and wasn't sleeping well, so neither was I (Mamas of little people, I feel your pain!). We had a toddler to take care of as well, and my husband was working lots to provide for our family. Though our families meant well, they were busy with their own lives at the time. I felt like I was drowning. I remember crying out to God frustrated and overwhelmed, not knowing where else to turn. As I cried out, things around me didn't change instantly, but I began to change. A transformation started to happen in my own heart when I surrendered my brokenness to God. I realized I didn't actually have all the answers, and I needed the Lord to lead my life.

As crazy as it sounds, it was in worshiping the Lord, that His mercy broke through. My perspective changed even though my situation hadn't. I found joy knowing that God was carrying me through this storm and had good plans for me ahead. I just needed to walk through the storm trusting and worshiping Him in the process.

God provided a beautiful group of bible study ladies to meet weekly with. That's where my faith grew. He worked on restoring my marriage and gave us wonderful family and friends to do life with. The Lord helped us raise our beautiful girls and even blessed us with a boy (who was a much better sleeper). He blessed our workplace and has been changing our hearts to find joy, even in the chaos life can bring. Had I not given my life over to the Lord, I don't know where I would even be today. Not here, that's for sure! All I can say is He is doing a much better job leading my life than I ever could! I know His plans for me are good. The blessings He provides daily are immeasurable, especially when I ask Him for help! It's crazy to think He had been pursuing me for so long, just waiting for me to open my heart to finally trust Him with my life. Even though my journey is never done until I am called home to be with my Saviour, I am forever learning, growing, and trusting Him more each step of the way.

I feel like we can hang on for dear life to everything we have ever known to be safe and comfortable. But only when we realize that it's not actually working our way anymore, do we finally let go and surrender. This is where we either sink or swim. And when we finally surrender our lives to the Lord and what He has in store for us, this is when the breakthrough happens. This is when we swim in the incredible blessings and freedom the Lord has for us.

Our lives are not our own, but what He has created you for, dear friend, is so much better than you could have ever dreamed of! Surrender the pain you are going through to Him. He knows that pain firsthand. He has redeemed you, so you could be set free to experience life and His goodness in full, even through the storms.

The process to healing is never easy, but the peace, joy, and freedom He brings is unexplainable. I remember the day I realized what it meant to experience true peace. Giving my life over to Him and trusting that His plans for me are good has brought me true peace. It's a daily choice to choose to follow Him, and every day He is there carrying me through.

> "...come back to God, your God, and obey him with your whole heart and soul according to everything that I command you today, God, your God, will restore everything you lost; he'll have compassion on you; he'll come back and pick up the pieces from all the places where you were scattered. No matter how far away you end up, God, your God, will get you out of there and bring you back to the land your ancestors once possessed. It will be yours again. He will give you a good life and make you more numerous than your ancestors."
> —Deuteronomy 30:1–5 MSG

His love is so great! He wishes for you to come to Him just as you are. He longs for you to surrender your will to His. He is waiting for you to seek Him and trust His promises for your life, so He can restore your heart and your home. Are you ready to let go, and trust the Lord?

Trusting Him doesn't mean you won't go through hard moments in your life, but it does mean you will have peace and victory in the process. He will wash you brand new and set your heart on fire. Life in abundance is waiting for you if you come before Him in all your hurt and shame, allowing Him to bring freedom from the pain that has bound you for so long. Nothing you have been through or have done can separate you from His great love for you. No more just surviving, my beautiful friend. It's time for you to thrive!

> *"Come now, let's settle this," says the LORD. "Though your sins are like scarlet, I will make them as white as snow. Though they are red like crimson, I will make them as white as wool."*
> —Isaiah 1:18 NIV

Prayer

Lord, I cannot do this life anymore. Please forgive me of all my wrongs. Please come into my heart and lead my life. I want all you have in store for me. Bring me to my full potential. In Jesus' name, amen!

COLOUR

Colour is all around us. It is everywhere we look, making our world come to life! How do you feel about colour? Are you attracted to a soft and neutral pallet? Or do you absolutely love bright and sunny colours? This may sound strange, but colours can really affect how we feel, stirring up different emotions for us. Colour can make you feel heavy and oppressed or it can uplift and inspire. It can demand your attention or be the perfect backdrop to bring the whole room together.

Colour either reflects, or absorbs light depending on what shade you choose. Darker tones tend to absorb the light making the room feel heavier, where lighter colours may reflect the light, leaving the room feeling brighter and lighter. Putting time and thought into the colours you choose for your space is super important, depending on the atmosphere you want to create.

To know just how important choosing your colours for your home can be, colours are chosen very strategically in marketing depending on what product or service is being sold. Companies choose their brand colours based on their desired demographics -who they want to sell their products or services to- drawing in the people who are most likely to purchase their product.

Fast food restaurants tend to use high contrast reds, oranges, and yellows to catch your eye as you drive past, stir up hunger, and create conversation for when you are sitting in the restaurant.

Hunting stores tend to keep their feel earthy and warm with lots of wood tones, cozy browns, and army greens to draw in their clients' love for the rugged outdoors. Likewise, a bridal shop decorated like the hunting store may not draw in a woman who is dreaming of her special day. Light and airy colours in soft pinks and creams may be more appealing to the bride choosing her elegant gown. Children's stores generally attract the playful side of kids with fun and bright colours to draw them in.

Thinking about your room right now, how do the colours make you feel? Peaceful and serene? Depressed and anxious? Invigorated? Joyful? Intimate?

To help achieve the feel you are after for your space, ask yourself a few questions. What will your room be used for? What is the design style you want to incorporate? Who will be spending time in there? What atmosphere do you want to create? Do you want it to feel warm and cozy? Clean and airy? Inspiring? Bright and playful?

Here are colours with some of the emotions they stir. They all come in various shades and depths.

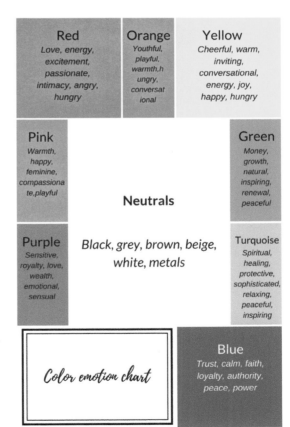

Lesson Seven: Rules in colour

Here are some rules to help create balance with colour for your redesign.

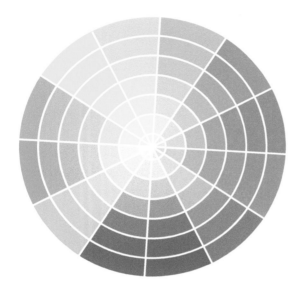

The colour wheel

The colour wheel

» Primary colours: red, blue, yellow. Any two of these colours combined creates secondary colours.
» Secondary colours: green, orange, purple. Any one of these colours blended with the primary colour next to it creates a tertiary colour.
» Tertiary colours: yellow orange, red orange, red violet, blue violet, blue green, yellow green.

Applying the colour wheel to your room design

» Complementary colours: Choose two colours directly opposite of each other on the colour wheel. Pairing complementary colours together creates a high contrast colour pallet, bringing the perfect balance of warm and cool together.

» Adjacent colours: Use any three colours that sit next to each other on the colour wheel.

» Split complementary: Any chosen colour combined with the two colours directly opposite it on the colour wheel, such as a true red paired together with a yellow green and a blue green.

Feel free to get creative here, but by using any of these colour combos in their equal shades, tones, tints or hues will help bring a perfect balance when choosing your room colours.

Colour intensities

Colours come in different shades, hues, tints, and values:

» Tint: a lighter version of a colour.
» Shade: a darker version of a colour.
» Tone: a softer more greyed version of a colour.
» Saturation or hue: the colour in its full brightness or intensity.

The more saturated colours pair well with whites and greys. They are cleaner feeling and thus need a cleaner feeling neutral.

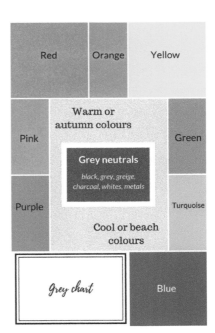

Grey and white tones can handle brighter colour hues

Browns need to be paired with softer shades of colours to work well together (Why? Maybe because browns have more pigment to them). Think warmer, more natural feeling colours.

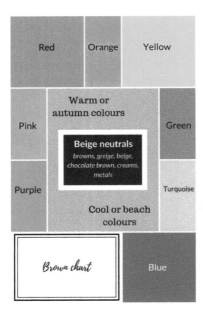

Browns and creams pair well with softer colour tones

Neutral Colours

Neutrals all have colour undertones as well that create an atmosphere based on the colour within it. When choosing a grey, know that grey is not just grey. It may have a purple undertone, or a brown undertone or even a blue feel to it. That's why your grey may look slightly blue when you get it on the wall. Even whites have undertones of colour within them.

There are many different colour tones running through neutrals. Be sure to choose a neutral that blends well with your fixed elements.

Lesson Eight: Choosing your colours

6:4:1 ratio or 6:4 ratio

Choose two or three colours you would like to incorporate into your redesign using the above guidelines, or any colour combinations that seem to work well together. Keep them all roughly similar hues (similar colour intensities of each other). Out of these colours, choose your main accent colour and use it roughly 6x in the space.

Add in your secondary colour, which may be used roughly 4x in the space. Then add in your third colour using it 2x in the space (if you want to incorporate a third colour). This third colour can be fun, adding in just a pop of that brighter accent colour you love without dominating the whole space.

You may vary the amount of times you use each colour but keep this ratio in mind. Equal amounts of each colour may result in competition between the colours, losing the peace you were after for your redesign! You always need one leading colour in the group, and the rest are there to support it, but still have equal importance to the design. There is a life metaphor for you!

You may have an art piece and an area rug with lots of beautiful colours, which is absolutely lovely, but only choose two or three colours from the pieces to use as your main accent colours. If you try to incorporate all the colours in the art throughout the space, it can quickly make the room feel overwhelming having too many colours all fighting for attention. Neutrals don't count in your main two or three colours.

Using the 6:4:1 scale: the turquoise accents in this room were roughly 60 per cent of the décor, the orange accents being 40 per cent, with pops of red roughly at 10 per cent. There were various warm greys through-out the room as well.

This room is a perfect example of the 6:4 ratio, with blue on the wall, the area rug, and the cushions, equaling to roughly 60 per cent of the décor. The yellow on the sofa and the artwork equals about 40 per cent of the décor. Notice the blue and yellow have equal values, but there are various shades of the blue and yellow for some depth and interest.

Neutrals

Neutrals are your whites, blacks, greys, browns, or creams. Try to use no more than two to three neutrals throughout the space. Keep your creams with browns; and whites with greys and blacks as much as possible.

Treat wood tones as neutrals, but they do need to be balanced throughout the space just like colour. Try not to use more than 2-3 different wood colours within the space. It also helps if there is a common undertone in the wood to tie the wood tones together. If it has an orange undertone, use various shades of orange undertone woods. If it has a yellow undertone, carry the yellow undertone in the rest of the woods.

Metals

Don't be afraid to use 2–3 metals to keep it interesting. Consistency is key to incorporating each element, so each metal you choose, use it throughout the space at least two times to make it look like it belongs there.

Monochromatic

Using a variation of lighter, medium, and darker versions of one colour in your space is called a monochromatic scheme. Lots of layers, textures, and patterns all in different shades of one colour is key to making this space cozy. You may choose to use one colour with some neutrals in this scenario, or this can work really great with a neutral scheme.

This is a softer toned green in a monochromatic pallet. Choose your colours to blend in with your inspirational fabric or artwork. Use it as a jumping off point for your redesign.

A neutral monochromatic living room

To choose the right colours for your own space, here are a few things to consider:

» **Look at your fixed elements**

Ignoring your existing wall colours for now, what colour are your fixed elements; such as flooring, tiles, cabinets and countertops? Are they on the brown side, grey side, cream or white? Determine your fixed element's undertones. Choose your paint colour in a similar undertone as your fixed elements. You want them to be cohesive and not to fight with each other. Nobody likes fighting, do they? Harmony is always better.

See how the paint colours blend into the fixed elements in the second picture?

Does this mean you are only committed to a brown wall if your fixed elements are brownish? Nope! You can introduce a cream with a beige undertone, or a beigey grey (like a griege) may even be a possibility. Hold a few large samples up to your fixed elements in natural lighting to be sure which options blend in the best.

»   **Look at what you wear.**

"Look! You're wearing blue. You look good in blue! You should surround your home with the colours that you look good in." I had a designer say to me a few years back. It's true; I have dirty blonde hair, blue eyes and fair skin. I do look better in cooler colours. This doesn't mean I can't pull off a lipstick red, but blue brings out my blue eyes. The funny thing is, I decorate my home with accents of blue. I totally cannot get enough of blues and turquoises.

I had a client tell me she absolutely didn't like green the moment I walked in the door. But guess what? She was wearing green! After exhausting all other colour options looking for the perfect paint colour for her walls, we landed on a soft green for her walls. And she was happy as pie. Why? Because she looked great in green! Look at your closet to help give you direction for your colour pallet.

This doesn't mean you have to put pink on your walls just because you wear a lot of pink, but this may be that you prefer brighter colour accents and will want to incorporate more playful colours into your space.

» **Inspirational pieces**

Another way to choose your colours for your redesign is to pull out your colours from a favorite quilt, throw pillow, rug, or art piece to incorporate on your walls and your accessories. Hold your paint samples against your favorite piece to find the right blend.

» **Compare your colours**

Tape a few possible paint samples against a white backdrop on the wall, in natural lighting. This gives you a clearer view to look at the colours without the existing wall color interfering. It also helps you compare each of the samples, while seeing the true undertones within them.

Now that you know how to choose your colours, let's apply them in your space.

How to create balance with your colour

» Colours, neutrals, and metals need to be used a variety of times throughout the space to create balance.

» Bright colours can be quite loud, so using them in accessories, rather than your fixed elements, makes it less costly to change out as trends change or you are ready for an update.

» If you love colour, don't be afraid to use it on your furniture, accessories, and walls.

» Choose timeless colour accents that don't require you to change your décor every year as colour trends change.

» Dark furniture carries weight, large bold patterns demand attention, and light coloured fabric can help a room feel light and airy.

» Try to use similar weights, textures, colours, and patterns throughout the space so one side doesn't look heavier or more tippy than the other side.

» Keep elements light and breezy in smaller areas. Larger areas can handle darker, richer, and bolder patterns, though it is fun to change this up depending on the look you are going for.

» In an open concept home, similar colour shades throughout your main areas help keep your home flowing and feeling cohesive.

» Choose your colours all at once to keep your home flowing as you go from room to room. The colours should all complement each other as you pair them side by side. You don't want any big scary surprises as you walk through your home. Use your top three complementary colours over and over, in various shades and accessories throughout your home.

Kids rooms or play rooms

Kids rooms or a playroom can be the exception to the rule from whatever is going on in the rest of the home. It should be their own domain and can be a fun surprise meant just for them. Kids love to play, and their room should reflect their likes and interests. Get them involved in the process so they feel invested, but don't be afraid to steer them a little or you could end up a little, well, over rainbowed!

Choose their bedding first. Then, pull out a complementary colour from the bedding keeping the above colour rules in mind.

If your kid is choosing a bright colour, and you don't want to commit to something quite so loud that may need to be repainted in a year or two, paint three walls in a neutral (such as an off white or soft greige), then paint their headboard wall with the brighter colour. This makes it easy to repaint later as their tastes change and/or as they grow up.

If you would like to paint all the walls the same colour, soften the shade to a slightly softer tone of the colour to keep it from overtaking the space. Four walls of one colour will bounce off each other, creating an even more intense version of that colour. We do want them to sleep at night after all...

My daughter a few years back wanted to paint her room pink. I chose a slightly softer version of the colour than what was in the quilt. (Imagine how bright it would have been otherwise?) Before I painted it, I asked her, "Are you sure you won't grow out of pink in a year or two?"

She was like "Nope, I love pink!" says the ten-year-old!

Sure enough, a year later, she was too cool for pink and wanted it turquoise. So, we sold the pink accessories to purchase more grown up turquoise ones, but the room remained pink not having the time or energy to paint it again quite so soon. Think up to five years ahead as you plan your child's room. Kids grow up so fast, and their tastes are forever changing.

Choose a more grownup feeling paint colour even if your child is young. It will last longer. Add in their favorite colours and characters with a few easy to change out accessories, rather than commit the whole bedroom to something super juvenile that they may call a "baby" room only a short year or two later.

Chapter
Five

IDENTITY

> *"God decided in advance to adopt us into his own family by bringing us to himself through Jesus Christ. This is what he wanted to do, and it gave him great pleasure."*
> —Ephesians 1:5 NLT

DO YOU KNOW WHO YOU ARE? I AM NOT TALKING ABOUT YOUR LIFE accomplishments or what you are good at. This is about what unique qualities make you, well, you! Not easy to define is it?

I would say I am passionate for people to find victory in their lives. The same victory I have personally experienced through Christ's redeeming love. I now know I am a child of God. My foundation is found in His promises He gave us in scripture. I love big, cry big, and celebrate big. But, I couldn't have said these things a few years back; I would have said I was anxious, stressed, unworthy, insecure, and clumsy. I felt like a failure wrapped up in finding other people's approval and what I accomplished. I was exhausted. I felt hurt trying to prove I was worthy to be loved. There was no way I felt confident enough to reach out to those around me, bound in the pain of my own hurts and insecurities. This can still be a battle that creeps up now and then, but it no longer defines my identity.

It took a lot of Godly counsel, spending time in the word of God, and following Jesus in obedience to find a breakthrough in my life. I found peace as my identity fell into place knowing I am loved by the one true King. I found freedom to live out my true purpose in Him!

Have you struggled to find your worth, never feeling quite "good enough"? Have you tried everything to prove your value, but ended up disappointed and hurt in the process? Have you struggled with anxiety and depression? Like chasing the wind, this world cannot satisfy. Nothing or no one can give you your worth but the One who created you to be beautiful you! There is peace in knowing this truth.

This is the paradigm shift right here. Are you ready for this? You are a child of the one true King! You become an heir to the throne when you accept His love and forgiveness for you. This is where you find your true identity.

You are beautiful, my friend. There is a greater plan and a purpose for your life. You are enough. You are worthy just the way you are. I pray you find rest in the Father's great love for you. This can be a hard truth to accept, especially if you have wounded, or been deeply wounded by the ones you love most. But, know there is a greater plan for your life when you live out your life in Christ. Let go of those lies you have held on to your whole life and choose to trust the truth of who you are in Jesus.

The King of Kings does not see your imperfections; He sees your heart. He sees you when you cry, when you ache, and where you have been deeply wounded. Let Him heal your heart and wrap you in His amazing unconditional love He has for you today. How? Read His word. Spend time in prayer. When your identity is wrapped in the one who created you, peace replaces the fear and anxiety, and joy comes to break through. It is a daily choice to stand firm on His promises of who you are. Give all your concerns and fears to Him, surround yourself with other people of faith you can worship and do life with. Live in obedience for the Lord and not to please man. This is where you find your true identity, my sweet friend.

Lay down the need to find happiness and approval, for happiness is only a temporary solution. Joy is eternal. Joy is what carries you throughout the beautiful and the difficult. How amazing it can be to feel the joy knowing you are loved, even in the painful moments! Trust His love for you. Nothing, absolutely nothing, we have done or experienced can separate us from His love for us, but it is up to you if you will receive the promises He has in store for you. So, lay down your cross and follow your Heavenly Father's promises for your life today.

> *My beloved spoke and said to me, "Arise, my darling, my beautiful one, come with me."*
> —Song of Songs 2:10 NIV

You are worthy. You are enough! You don't have to prove anything. Just be. Rest in the Lord and just be beautiful you.

WHO AM I?

What lies have I believed about myself?	
What makes me unique?	
Who does Christ say I am?	
Phrase of truth about who I am	

ARTWORK

Artwork can be an amazing tool for pulling together the feel of your interior design. It can tell your story and set the mood for the whole space. Art may be used to accent features of the home by drawing our eyes to the desired focal points. It can also be a great way to incorporate your lovely accent colours. The size and height of your art can also help bring balance to the space, so being strategic in how you hang the pieces you choose is important to creating a clean, cozy, inviting space.

Look around at your walls in your space right now. How does it feel? Is it hung too high? Is it dated? Is it too small for the wall? Do your walls feel empty and cold? Does your room feel slightly cluttered with many random pieces hung just anywhere? This can make our house feel messier than it is, and really, who wants a messier home when keeping a clean home can be difficult enough?

Lesson Nine: How to hang art

There are a few things to remember when hanging art to create a cozy atmosphere. Let's start with the colour of your artwork …

Colour and style

Colours can create balance within the space as we chatted about in the previous chapter, so choosing art for your room that relates to the colours and style going on in the space is key. All your pieces should all have a similar feeling throughout the room. If you have a beachy feeling room, place similar coloured beachy feeling art on the walls.

My home currently is a modern farmhouse style. I really could use any style of art with my neutral walls and flooring, but the vintage farmhouse signs I have chosen helps pull together the story I wanted to create.

My sister looked around my room as she was visiting one day and said, "Your walls are so bossy!" Ha-ha, sisters! She was joking. She really does love the look in my home, and I love the "bossy" reminder they give us every day.

If you have an open concept room, you could get away with slightly different themed art from area to area; but do keep your colours and style similar so they make sense being in the same room together.

When artwork is placed above a piece of furniture, it should tie together with similar colours below to create one unit.

This is a focal point I created in a dining room. The frame around the mirror relates to the colour of the knobs. It also matches the dark dining table in the room, so everything looks like it belongs together.

Scale

We chatted about creating a focal point in the previous chapter, but one of the key ingredients to drawing your eye to your focal point in your space is the scale of the artwork. If the piece has enough impact, it will help draw your eyes where you want them to go. Assess the size and shape where you will place your art. Is it more square or rectangular? Is it quite a large area? Hold up your art in place. How does it look there? Does it feel cozy and inviting? Does it feel like the right shape for the space? Do the colours relate to the rest of the room and the furniture below it? Is it large enough to draw your eye to your focal point? Or, does it feel lost and too small for the area?

If the space is more square feeling, use a square or round piece for that location. If it feels more rectangular, use a rectangular piece, or put two pieces together to create more of a rectangle. If it's a large area, use a larger piece of art or an arrangement of a few similar pieces all hung together to create the feeling of one large art piece. Hang them two to three inches apart on the wall.

The space above this sofa is best in the form of a rectangle. Here are a few arrangements that would all work great. Add a lamp on either side and this living room's focal point would be complete.

If your artwork feels too small for the wall, use what you have by bringing a few pieces together to create a more scaled focal point.

The area above this dining table was too big for just one piece of art. By placing two pieces of art side by side, it created enough of a focal point to draw your eye to the dining area which helps define the space. The vignette is tied together with the colour of the artwork matching the black furniture below it.

Height

Height is also very important when hanging your artwork, as it can quickly appear as if its floating or lost if it's hung too high. Bringing your artwork down a few inches can make all the difference to making your space feel cozy and inviting, while tying your furniture and art together as one vignette.

This piece of art is scaled large enough for the wall. Hung low enough at just the right height, creates a focal point all on its own. This art also has similar accent colours to the rest of the room, making it pleasing for your eyes.

Keys to hang your artwork correctly

» If you are hanging art in an open concept room, create a focal point for each designated area, then add in your secondary focal points with your art.

» Place your art centred above the item below.

» Don't hang art on a wall smaller than two feet or it can create a cluttered feeling.

» Small wall space around the focal points need not be filled, or it can take away from the impact of the focal points. Our eyes need a place to rest and breathe to take in the areas of interest you have worked so hard to create.

» Hang artwork that fits the shape and size of the wall you are hanging it on.

» Use art that relates to the other colours, furniture, and style in the room

» The artwork on the wall should be roughly 60–80 per cent of the size of what is below it.

» If your area is quite large, try two larger similar pieces of art hung side by side, or create a gallery of pieces hung in an imaginary square or rectangle to fill the space.

» For a wall with no furniture below the art, use art that is roughly 60-80 per cent of the wall space you are using to create enough impact with your art.

» Artwork should be hung roughly around 5–10" from the bottom of the art piece to the top of furniture below it so they make a visual connection.

» Hang your artwork roughly six feet from the floor to the top of your art. If it's a larger piece, it may be hung slightly higher than six feet to the top of your art. If it's a smaller piece, it may need to be slightly lower than six feet to the top of your piece … but you get the idea. If you have really high ceilings, don't hang your artwork any higher, you just may need larger more dramatic pieces to feel scaled in the large space.

This may sound like a funny analogy, but the art you hang on your wall is almost like comparing it to an outfit. Your shirt needs to relate in some way to the pants you choose to wear to create balance and harmony.

Likewise, if you are wearing a dress, you don't need any pants unless your dress is too short. So, if you don't have furniture below your piece, your art needs to be large enough to balance itself out on the wall, or it could look slightly well … naked.

Now you know the rules to hanging your art on your wall, so let's get it on the wall using these steps:

1. Remove all your artwork from your walls in your room.
2. Find your main focal point wall.
3. Choose your desired piece of art and hold it up there. You may need an assistant to help you with this or prop it up on your table or sofa (carefully so it doesn't fall!).
4. Step back and see how your piece looks with the rest of the space. How are your size, height, and colours all tying together?
5. When your focal point is found, hold up your art for your supporting walls, resisting the urge to hang art on the small walls. Create a secondary focal point on each available wall. Plan out your art in the room before you hang just in case you need to reconfigure it a bit.
6. When you are happy with the location for your art, hold it up to find the right height. Make a small mark on the wall using a pencil along the top of the picture.
7. Turn the art over and measure the distance from the hook or wire pulled tightly, to the top of the picture frame. Add that measurement down from your pencil mark.
8. Make a small pencil mark at the new height on the wall.
9. Measure across the wall to find the centre of the space and make a small mark there.
10. Double check your measurements.
11. Make a mark where the height and width match up, and hammer in your hook or nail on that mark.
12. Hang your piece of art, step back and enjoy.

How to create a gallery wall

» Collect an arrangement of art, inspirational words, and an array of special family photos in fun frames.

» Arrange all these pieces on the floor with 2–3 inches between each piece until your happy with the arrangement. Take a picture of your arrangement so you remember what it looks like.

» Starting at the centre of your large open wall, hang your centre piece first and build out from there. This is a fun wall, so it need not be perfect. Just remember to not hang this arrangement too high on your wall.

Chapter
Six

PURPOSE

> *"Serve wholeheartedly, as if you were serving the Lord, not people."*
> —Ephesians 6:7 NIV

SO, FRIEND, NOW YOU KNOW WHO YOU ARE IN THE FATHER'S EYES, BUT you may still have a hard time believing you are worthy of His love. Knowing you are loved gives you the confidence to move forward in the true purpose you were created for. You have a God-given plan for your life, and nothing, not one single thing in your life is wasted when you live your life for Christ.

You have been created for such a day as this, so be brave, my friend. Allow the Lord to use your story for His glory. Your story is important to reach out to others in their broken moments. You are not some silly person brought into this world by accident. There is a reason you were created beyond your own desires, mistakes, or what other people have labeled you to be. Hard to believe, isn't it? Especially, if you have been told otherwise.

I know, I get it! The Lord is using every one of my experiences to reach out and help others going through similar situations. He broke down my pride, showed me His grace, while giving me grace for others in the process. Nothing, not one moment, has been wasted as I am learning to trust Jesus with my life.

Bill Wilson spent many years battling alcohol. He finally became a recovering alcoholic when he gave his life to Christ. Desperately trying to stay sober, he found freedom from his disease as he spent time talking to other alcoholics. Finding purpose for his life helped keep him sober. Little did he know he would co-found the well-known recovery program called AA, Alcoholics Anonymous. His pain and brokenness brought freedom to so many others going through a similar struggle! His wife, Lois, in all the pain she experienced living with her alcoholic husband, created the group Al-Anon – a support group for those going through the struggles of watching their loved ones stuck in this devastating disease. They found freedom as they lived out their new-found faith while reaching out to serve others.

My friend, you have a calling on your life today. What you have experienced can and will be used for more, if you're willing. Your story doesn't have to die in the pain of what you are going through. You may be used to encourage someone else going through what you have gone through. It's what you do with your story that matters. Rise up, beautiful one, to find healing so you can come alongside others to find victory. Help others learn from your mistakes so they don't have to go through what you have experienced, or at least meet them in the broken places to know there is hope. Understanding the Father's deep sacrifice for us is often enough to compel us forward to reach into the broken world around us, taking our eyes off our own painful circumstances to find freedom from what we are experiencing ourselves.

You don't even have to strive to find your purpose! What are your passions? When you think of helping people who are hurting, who comes to mind? Who or what drives you to serve others? It's usually what we are most passionate about is where our purpose lies. Start small by looking around you. Who are the people in your life, workplace, school or neighbourhood? Do you see a need? Serve them in love.

Keep healthy boundaries as you do though. Remember your oxygen mask? You still need to be filled to be able to pour into someone else.

How are you doing, my sweet friend? Ready to reach out? By reaching out to your neighbours (the people in your area of influence in your everyday life), we can quickly make a difference in this world… one person at a time. We become filled with joy knowing we were made for more. Serving somehow breaks the dark cloud around us and brings us to a place of thanksgiving and worship. Not sure about this? Try it.

Do something for someone without expecting anything in return. When we serve from our passions, it takes our eyes off our own problems and brings us purpose. It also touches people's hearts deeper than we could ever know. Joy bubbles out of us as we reach into the lives around us. But, we can't do this on our own strength. We need the transforming power of God to fill us with strength and worship, so we can be all we were created to be. As we move forward in our purpose, even greater blessing and clarity begins to unfold in our lives. Confidence will rise as you move forward in your purpose, dear friend.

Prayer

Lord, help me to understand your great love for me, so I can reach into the needs around me. Help me to live out my greater purpose in your strength and joy so I can be used for your glory. In Jesus' name, amen.

ACCESSORIES

Accessories are the fun part of the redesign process, bringing the whole vision together. Accessories can be super overwhelming to know how to style them. Done wrong, they can leave your room feeling cluttered and messy. Arranged just right, these final touches can transform your space, hiding all the imperfections.

Lesson Ten: How to accessorize your space

Accessories are another great way of incorporating your accent colours or special pieces that have meaning to you. Don't try to use every accessory you own; but do use a few key pieces to help tell the story you are trying to create.

Accessories can help hide a multitude of sins. If you have a fireplace or a sofa you would love to change, but don't have the option to change it, try adding a few fun accessories to freshen it up and distract your eyes.

Think of your furniture like an ice cream sundae, (Yup, I really do love my sweet treats). You can eat ice cream without any toppings and it will still taste good, but adding in a few yummy toppings helps elevate the flavours and interest of the ice cream.

You can't add just any kind of toppings either, as not all toppings work well together (Seriously have you ever eaten your kid's ice cream mixed with chocolate, sour candies and gummy worms? Yuck!). By blending a few flavours that work well together, your sweet treat will be a yummy experience. Think of your accessories like the ice cream toppings in your room. They give your eyes a sweet experience, making it easy to change out if you want a slightly different taste or a seasonal flavour.

Accessories for a whole room can be just as costly as furniture to purchase but are equally important to pulling the décor together. Accessories can be one of the simplest and most cost-effective ways to make changes to your room without having to do expensive renovations. If you are using accessories you already own, add in the pieces that work within your vision and leave the ones that don't. Try them elsewhere in your home, but if they don't work in your other spaces, don't be afraid to let them go or get creative with them. That said, I do have a cabinet with a small amount of extra décor hidden away that I rotate through for each season or as trends change.

Size

» A variety of different sized accessories creates interest. In a larger room, think big! You need a variety of quite large accessories to make the impact your large room needs.

» Smaller rooms can handle smaller accessories if they are mixed with a few slightly larger pieces to create interest.

» If we display a bunch of little items we have on hand, it quickly creates clutter. Be strategic with how you arrange your accessories by incorporating a variety of small, medium and large elements all layered together to build one pretty vignette.

Style

» The feel of your accessories should match the style and story of the design scheme you are creating.

» Use accessories that work with your colour scheme.

» If you have a collection of accessories you want to incorporate, use only the pieces that are your absolute favourites, have similar colours, or suits the style of your space.

» Use a combination of vintage and new accessories to give your space some character. Old pieces tell a story. New accessories create a fresh feel.

Balance

» Whatever is done on one side of a vignette needs to be balanced on the other side with similar heights. Look at it like a triangle. The centre being the tallest, arrange all the pieces coming down from there by incorporating different textures, elements, and colours to create interest and a layered effect.

» Create formality by placing similar items on both sides of the triangle. This is great in a formal dining room or living room.

» Create a relaxed look with different pieces on either side but in similar heights.

Odd numbers

»   Use odd numbers in different heights, colours, and elements to create interest. Use odd numbers in your floral arrangements as well. I am not quite sure why this is, but somehow the imperfectness is more pleasing to look at than when everything is perfectly symmetrical. We get the symmetrical through the balance of colours and heights throughout the space.

»   Arranging a set of two in the same or different heights can be done as well.

Vignette

» Create an area of interest or a focal point for a pretty display.

Tablescapes

Following the accessories guideline, create a centrepiece in the middle of your dining table or coffee table.

» If it's a square or round table, divide the centre of your table into an imaginary square or triangle. Place a piece, or layers of pieces within each section using an arrangement of different heights, textures, and colours.

» If you have a rectangular table, break it into two or three imaginary sections lengthwise across the centre of your table and layer the same way as above. Use two or three of the same item for a more symmetrical look.

Lighting

» Lighting can be a huge component to add interest, ambiance, and balance to the space. Think of your room like an elegant cocktail dress; without adding jewelry, your dress may feel like just another dress, but add jewelry, it elevates the dress, which helps set the tone for the evenings formality. Your lighting can do just this, by setting the feel you are after for your room.

Area Rugs

» An area rug defines the space while adding texture. Your area rug should be large enough to place at least the front feet (if not all the feet) of your seating on the rug if possible. Area rugs can also be a great way to incorporate your accent colours.

Throw pillows and blankets

» Throw blankets and pillows add much texture, helping your room feel layered and cozy. Incorporate your colours and neutrals in your pillows, as well as a combination of geometric, stripes, textures, and patterns. The throw blanket should carry one or more of your accent pillow colours to help tie it into your display of serious cozy.

Styling Shelving

» Shelves can be dust collectors, but styled just right, they can be a great way to display some of your favourite pieces. Don't think of it as a place for storage, but more like a display. This will help keep you from cluttering up your shelving over time with "stuff".

To style your shelving, pull everything off your shelves, then layer a variety of different textures, heights, and your accent colours throughout the shelves. Keep it simple allowing breathing room around your pieces. Don't stack them too full, even if you have lots of books. Books can be stacked in short stacks propped up with a basket or a vase beside them or laying down with an ornamental item on top. This can be a good time to downsize your book collection. Keep the heavier pieces on the lower shelves with some of the lighter items near the top. Play around until it feels balanced. It's kind of like a puzzle and can be fun to play around with until it feels just right.

Accessory Elements

Use a variety of these elements in your accessories throughout your space, while keeping your design style and colours in mind.

»   Metals. Use up to two or three different metal finishes but try not to use more than this. Be sure to repeat them somewhere within the space so they look intentional.
»   Glass vases, bottles, or candle holders.
»   White can be key in freshening up a space. If your room feels heavy, incorporate more white accessories within the scheme.
»   Use nature. Greenery and/or florals and/or wood add life to any room.
»   Lighting or lamps create balance and ambiance.
»   Candles with candle holders are another great way to incorporate ambiance for the evening. Candle holders are an easy way to add your accent colours.
»   Small stacks of books. They tell a "story".
»   Collections you love, or special heirlooms.
»   Throws and accent pillows.
»   Vases.
»   Décor boxes or baskets.
»   Pretty frames with special memories or family members. Don't have too many of these on display but a few can feel inviting.
»   Jars or special dishes that work with your redesign.

What are some accessories you would add to this list?

How to create a styled vignette

1.   Start with your largest art in the centre. This could be a piece of art, a mirror, a clock, or metal wall art.
2.   Add in a medium-sized accent piece to each side to create balance.
3.   If your vignette is a large enough area, add in shorter accessories layered within the outer corners to complete the triangle.
4.   If you still have room, add in two more even smaller accessories to polish off the layered effect.

Think three, five or seven items depending on the size of your vignette to create your imaginary triangle.

Don't be afraid to play around with your accessories until it looks just right. Are you wondering how you will know if it looks right? My eyes are trained, but before long, yours will be too! This just takes some practice and playing around with your pieces. Don't take this too seriously. Throw on some good music and play around with what you have. Leave it and come back with fresh eyes to make some more adjustments as needed. Look through the lens of your camera if you're not sure. Somehow the eyes of the camera cannot lie and tends to reveal what needs to be adjusted. Change it up from time to time, or even seasonally, if you want. This is the fun of accessories.

Bring it home

» **Entryway**

Add a few fun accessories like lamps and greenery, or a floral arrangement to your console table. Art or a mirror on the wall will finish off your invitation to come on in.

» **Living room**

Get some big fluffy accent pillows and a throw for your sofa, a large area rug, and some big table lamps on your end tables. A few accessories on your coffee table will polish it off.

» **Master bedroom**

A fluffy duvet, throw pillows, and a throw blanket on your bed alongside large table lamps on your bedside tables. Add in a cozy chair or two in the corner to curl up in. Finish it off with candles, a floral arrangement, or a few good books ready to read, stacked beside your bed.

» **Office**

Create pretty storage. Use baskets if you need to hide things on shelves. Add inspiring art on the wall, and a cozy throw on an accent chair for an extra reading corner.

» **Dining room**

Some floral arrangements or greenery on your dining table, lamps and accessories on a buffet with large artwork on the wall to create your focal point. Add in curtains, and a table runner for texture. An area rug in your accent colours is optional, depending on what is more functional for your busy family.

Chapter
Seven

ENTERTAINING

> *"As Jesus and the disciples continued on their way to Jerusalem, they came to a certain village where a woman named Martha welcomed him into her home. Her sister, Mary, sat at the Lord's feet, listening to what he taught. But Martha was distracted by the big dinner she was preparing. She came to Jesus and said, 'Lord, doesn't it seem unfair to you that my sister just sits here while I do all the work? Tell her to come and help me.' But the Lord said to her, 'My dear Martha, you are worried and upset over all these details! There is only one thing worth being concerned about. Mary has discovered it, and it will not be taken away from her.'"*
> —Luke 10:38–42 NLT

DO YOU ENJOY ENTERTAINING? OR DO YOU FIND IT A BIT STRESSFUL?

Maybe you love entertaining, but life feels too busy or expensive to have people over. Some people really do have a gift for hosting and some don't enjoy it. That's okay! The Bible talks about having a Mary heart. I feel like no matter where your strengths lie, we are all called to have a Mary heart where we sit and rest at the feet of Jesus. Where we can stop and enjoy Him, taking time to breathe with the ones around us without being distracted by all the details.

We are called to love our neighbours. Hospitality is a great way to love when our world is slowly becoming less and less relational. We actually crave relationship. People will never remember your home was perfectly clean or perfectly decorated, but they will remember your hospitality and that you enjoyed your time with them.

I went with a couple of friends to a lady's home a couple of years back. This was a lady we had never met before. We were invited in, coffee ready, with some amazing store-bought treats purchased just for us. I felt so honoured and special! Every day, promptly at 2 p.m. the door was open for coffee and good conversation to anyone who wanted to come by. Her home was small and quaint, but the fireplace was lit with a place to sit. This moment shifted my priorities to realize it doesn't have to be perfect. I just need to be willing to open the door of my heart and my home to those around me. Whether it is resting at the feet of Jesus or sitting with the ones we love over yummy tea and conversation; making room to open our doors to those around us is essential. Let's keep it simple and refocus on what really matters.

> *"Love the Lord your God with all your heart and with all your soul and with all your mind and with all your strength. The second is this: 'Love your neighbor as yourself.' There is no commandment greater than these."*
> —Mark 12:30–31 NIV

Going into entertaining with this mindset, I pray it releases you to take things a little less seriously, open your door, and just hang out and embrace the imperfect. But, how can you do that when you have all the prep involved with entertaining? Well, let's make the process a little simpler for you.

Lesson Eleven: How to make entertaining simple

I love entertaining, but I used to try to make the whole experience perfect. I felt like I had to prove something to myself and my company. By the time my guests came over, I was way too tired to enjoy them! I have since realized it's not about performing, it's about creating time for the people we have over. Since time is not something I feel like I have a lot of right now, here is a simple process I use for every party I throw, big or small.

Simple steps to entertaining for a party or gathering

1. Get inspired.

    Pictures on social media or a good ol' cookbook helps me to get inspired.
2. Make a guest list.

    Always over invite as there are usually a few that cancel last minute. Decide on a day and time and invite via social media, email, text, phone … so many options these days, right?
3. Make a menu.

    Decide what you want your guests to bring, or if you are going to make it all. I am a firm believer in pot luck style to make the load light. Most people want to help anyways.
4. Make a list.

Make a list of everything you need for your party including groceries and decorations. It helps you to stay organized. Refer to your inspirational pictures if needed. Check off what you already have in the house. Doing this saves so much time when you go to the grocery store instead of guessing what you need.

5. Go shopping.

Shop for your list a couple of days before.

6. The day before.

Clean up and prep as much as you can the day before, to take some of the stress off and leave you with more energy to enjoy your guests.

7. Assemble the last touches.

The day of the party, finish off the final touches of cleaning, decorating, and the food prep. If you have helpers in your house, recruit as much help as possible by giving everyone a job. Or, invite a friend to help to lighten your load and have some fun working together.

8. Get yourself ready.

9. One hour before.

Assemble the final touches. Put out your drinks and get the coffee and tea ready. Create the mood with fun lighting, candles, music, etc. Set out food when ready to eat.

10. Open your door. Not so bad, right?

I feel a call to open our doors and get to know the people around us again. We simply don't have time anymore, but do you know what? We don't have time not to. This is what we are here for! We need to shift our priorities by letting go of the crazy of life in our schedules. Life does have its seasons and not every season will be the easiest to open our doors, but we can pray to have the opportunity with time to rest to be there for those who need some love.

If this process still feels tiresome and complicated, here are some of my easy button tips. Everyone should have an easy button in their back pocket, right?

My secret easy entertaining tips and tricks.

» Buy colour-coordinated napkins, paper plates, cups, and utensils to always have on hand for easy no dishes cleanup!
» Pop up a cute banner that you have on hand, ready to hang for the party.
» Do a buffet style potluck dinner, easy pre-purchased food, or even healthy take-out.
» Ask for help. Some of our favorite moments have been in the kitchen as a family all cooking and cleaning up together. But when the kids were little, it was just better they were not around (they can be more work than help at that stage, right?). Ask a friend or a spouse to help you with the kids, if needed, so you can get the party ready.

And if entertaining still sounds stressful to you, meet somewhere like a restaurant, a local beach, or even grab healthy take-out and have a picnic in the park. This way you can all enjoy yourselves, be present, and then go home when you're done! It is more important that we spend time building relationships with those around us.

REDESIGN

Here is where we bring all our lessons together by finally applying them to your space. Go get some comfy clothes on, grab your tape measure and a pencil, and begin the transformation. Refer back to the lessons as needed as you begin the hands-on design process.

Lesson Twelve: The redesign process

» **Get inspired**

Find some magazines and pics online that inspire you. Narrow it down to three or four of your favourite images.

» **Choose your room to redesign**

I will be referring to your living room, but you can apply these steps in any room. Make it simple by focusing on one room at time. Maybe this will inspire you to do every room in your home!

» **Answer these questions**

Feel free to write out your answers here in the book; or grab a cute notebook you can make notes in and take shopping with you.

Which room do you want to redesign?

What don't you like about your space?

What do you love about your space?

What do you love about your inspirational pictures?

What colours do you want to incorporate into your redesign?

What style is your home currently?

What style do you want to incorporate into your home?

What are the needs for your space?

What needs to stay in this room? Why?

What doesn't work and needs to go? Why?

Is there a piece from another room you could try?

What is your budget to work with?

Which is your inspirational piece to build your design around?

» **Plan your layout**.

Measure your room and draw it out on graph paper. Cut out your furniture pieces to scale. Find your room's focal point and arrange your furniture around it. Keep the layout guidelines in mind as you play around with your furniture. Create good balance within the room and a good flow of space. Do you need to change or eliminate any of your existing furniture to make the space flow better? Play around with your furniture on the floor plan until it flows, functions, and feels balanced within the space.

» **Create your inspiration board**

On a clean white sheet of paper, add in a picture of each piece of furniture you want to incorporate including your inspirational piece. Add in a picture of your fixed elements and any colours you would like to use. Add in your accessories. Play around by adding and removing each piece until it feels right. Compare it to your inspirational pictures. What needs to be adjusted to create your desired look? Keep adjusting as needed until you feel good about your vision for your redesign. This doesn't have to be perfect as it may can be adjusted slightly when you place the items in the room; it just helps you anchor where you take your redesign.

Planning done! Let's play!

» **Remove everything from your room**

Leaving only your major furniture pieces such as sofas, bed, dining table, or desk, take everything else out of your room to create a blank canvas to work with.

» **Rearrange your furniture**

Arrange your large furniture pieces as planned in your room layout. Don't be afraid to play around until the furniture feels good, flows, and functions well, even if it's not exactly as you planned. Keep your heights, colours, and weights balanced throughout the space. If you have an area rug, you can add it in now and arrange your furniture around it. Will this layout function for your everyday living?

» **Add in your accent furniture**

Time to add in your accent furniture such as your end tables, shelving, and chairs. Again, don't be afraid to shift them around until they flow well and are pleasing to your eyes. Try pieces from other rooms in your house if needed. Get creative here.

By now your space should feel defined, drawing your eye to the main focal point of the room.

Does it feel balanced? Does one side of the room feel heavier than the other? What can be added or rearranged? Do you need to add in or take away a piece of furniture? Or just rearrange your existing furniture slightly to create the necessary balance in the room?

» **Hang your art**

Try your art on your focal point first. Grab art from other rooms in your home to try if needed. Next, add art on your other walls centred within the desired spaces. Play around with your art until the room feels balanced. If you're still not sure, arrange your accessories before making any final decisions.

Use artwork that works within the colour scheme and tells the story you want to create. Don't be afraid to leave the smaller walls empty or give space around your vignettes. This gives your eyes a rest, drawing your eyes to the pretty features in the room. If you find that your existing art just isn't working, you can add new art to your wish list.

» **Accessorize your room**

Time to play with your accessories. This part is like a puzzle. Don't be afraid to try a few options keeping the guidelines in mind. Even though there are rules in interior design, it's art and getting creative within the guidelines is a must! Your room is like a canvas. Be intentional in your design decisions so it feels like all the pieces belong there and are not just an afterthought.

Let go of the pieces that didn't make it into the space. See if they work in another room in your home. If they don't, bring them to a thrift store, or try to sell them to help pay for new accessories.

Take a step back and look around. You did it!

» **How does it feel?**

Look around your newly-redesigned space and ask yourself these questions;

- Is there a balance of colour, heights, textures, and accessories throughout the space?
- Are your eyes drawn to the pretty features in the room?
- Do you feel invited in?
- Is it easy to walk in and throughout the space?
- Are there any further adjustments needed to make your redesign feel balanced?
- Are there any room updates needed to make the space feel complete?

Feel free to adjust, add, or take away as time goes on, until it feels good and works well. I am forever changing and readjusting my own space. It's part of the fun of decorating. Don't get discouraged if your space doesn't feel perfect. Redesign takes some practice, but the more practice you get, the better you will be at pulling your rooms together. Trends change, life changes, and so do our needs, so change up your redesign every so often to keep your home feeling decluttered, fresh and updated.

» **Update list**

Your room may be perfect now and that's great! But chances are you are noticing a few things that may need updating whether it's a new area rug, painting your coffee table, or a fresh colour on your walls.

Maybe you need something simple like a few new accent pillows or artwork. Make a list of your desired DIYs' and shopping list. Don't feel stressed to purchase or do any projects right away. This will give you a plan to move forward with as you have time or money, helping take your redesign to the next level if you so desire.

List of to do projects

List of items to purchase

Wish list

Shopping

If you have a shopping budget, a little can go a long way. Do over buy when shopping for accessories as you will use more than you planned on, and you can return what does not work. If you can't decide which designer throw to purchase, go ahead and buy five throws, then return the ones that don't work in your home. With that many options one is bound to work, right?

If you are creative, the thrift stores can have some sweet treasures at very sweet prices too. Having a mixture of old and new pieces creates more of a story than a whole pile of expensive store-bought items anyways.

Shopping for accessories.

» Create your budget
» Take your list and inspiration board with you as you go shopping.
» Carry around paint chips of your colours as you shop to get the right coloured accessories.
» If you are shopping and are unsure which items to choose, even with referring to the inspiration board, don't be afraid to take a few viable options home with you (if the décor store has a good return policy) and bring back the ones that don't work.

Shopping for furniture

» If you are looking for some new pieces of furniture and you have a decent budget to work with, browse online, or at your local furniture stores to try out new pieces that may work for you. Get cozy on the furniture to know if it is comfortable for your everyday needs. Compare the colour of the furniture with your paint samples.
» Take pictures of any favourites that may work within your vision.
» Measure the furniture to know it will fit in your space and through your doorways.
» Narrow down your options to what fits within your function and budget.
» Place it onto your inspiration board to make sure it works within your vision.
» Once you have narrowed down your decision, ask if you can bring a fabric sample or a cushion home with you. Our home lighting can really alter the appearance of colours.
» Purchase the desired items. Talk pricing with your furniture supplier as most furniture places are willing to give you somewhat of a deal if you ask them. At the very least, maybe you can get the delivery for free?

Staging

The principles found in this book can make your staging process simple if you ever need to sell. The only difference between redesigning your home and staging for selling, is keeping it a little less personal for selling by removing personal photos and opening up the space with minimal furniture to show off the features of your home. Homeowners need to envision themselves in the home and not feel like they are walking through your personal home. Stage each room for what it was meant for by making the dining room a dining room, an office into an office (not the playroom), and the bedrooms into bedrooms (not a storage room). Keep it impersonal with neutral colours to appeal to more possible homebuyers.

This room was redesigned to be staged for selling. We rearranged the existing furniture and accessories to create focal points for each area, painted the walls in a neutral colour, and then added a couple new throw pillows on the sofas to freshen up the space.

You can do this, my beautiful friend! You can redesign your own space and it will be lovely. Just have fun and enjoy the process. Life is all about the journey, and we are never done. Your space is the same way. Does it need to be magazine worthy? Nope! You just need to find peace in your home and contentment within your heart to enjoy what you have been blessed with.

RECIPES

Some of my favourite recipes

Our family is changing rapidly as our kids get older. I feel like I am afraid to blink, or they will already be out the door! The years of raising our kids have gone fast (even though sometimes it feels super slow), so capturing these last few moments with them has become even more important. With our Mennonite background, every special moment somehow seems to revolve around food (this makes it really difficult to stick to a diet…). As we create memories with those around us, here are a few simple, old fashioned, go-to recipes that help make entertaining yummy and memorable.

I love fresh, homemade, natural ingredients, full of protein and loads of veggies to give your body sustaining energy. To live a balanced life, we cannot forget about a few yummy treats of course. They just make life a little sweeter with something to look forward to, don't they? What are some of your family favourites?

Homemade portabella mushroom soup

I had to try this recipe as my husband loves mushrooms. This is a simple one pot recipe that actually tastes even more amazing the next day.

Chop finely, and sauté together on medium heat in a large pot until the sweet aromas rise, and the garlic and onion become translucent:

- » 2 cups chopped baby bella mushrooms (I use the prepackaged baby porta-bella mushrooms)
- » 1 tbsp. avocado oil or olive oil
- » 1 onion
- » ½ head of garlic

Make a roué by whisking together in the same pan (push the mushroom mixture off to the side):

- » 2 tbsp. butter melted
- » ¼ cup flour

Once the butter and flour are blended together (it will form a ball), whisk in:
- » 2 cups chicken broth
- » 1 cup milk (I use almond milk as a great dairy substitute)

Add in to taste:
- » Sprinkle of salt and pepper
- » ½ tsp thyme
- » 1 tsp parsley

Bring pot to a boil while stirring occasionally. Let simmer 5-7 mins. Take off heat and stir in:
- » ½ cup heavy cream (Coconut cream could work here as well)
- » 1–2 tsp soy sauce

Top with parsley and parmesan cheese. Serve with seasoned grilled chicken breasts and yummy crusty bread on the side. Serves about 4.

Hearty chicken noodle soup

Place 4–6 large raw chicken breasts or 6–8 chicken thighs (frozen or thawed) in a large pot (I used an 8.5 quart pot). Add in 2 cups chicken broth and fill the rest of the pot with water until the pot is about three-quarters full.

Bring the water to a boil. Bring temp down to simmer until chicken is fully cooked. While this is simmering, prep your veggies.

When chicken is fully cooked, use a slotted spoon to pull out chicken and shred using two forks. Set chicken aside. Add the following finely chopped veggies to the broth:

» 4 stalks celery
» 4 large peeled carrots
» 1 white onion
» 2 cups corn
» 2-3 cloves garlic

Bring back to a boil. Once at a boil, turn temp down to simmer for about 10 minutes or until veggies are just starting to soften.

Add the chicken back to the pot and these spices to taste:

» 1 tsp ginger
» ¼ cup dried parsley
» Salt and pepper to taste
» ½ tsp star anise
» 2 tsp garlic seasoning
» 1 bay leaf or 1 tsp rubbed bay
» Chicken bouillon to taste (about 1 tbsp. or 2 more if needed)

Bring pot to a boil on high again and add in noodles:

» 14 oz steam fried noodles or one small package of pasta

Turn down temp to med/high. Stir often until noodles are fully cooked.

Take off heat. Serve with fresh Grandma's buns or sourdough bread.

Serves a small party of people around 12–14 people. Your house will smell amazing! Warm up on the stove to serve the next day if needed.

Grandma's buns

With a few revisions as this recipe was passed down from generation to generation, they remind me of home. The most wonderful feeling was walking into the house after a busy day at school to find these buns ready for us to enjoy, or helping Grandma roll them into delicious cinnamon buns. These fluffy, slightly sweet, melt in your mouth buns accompany the homemade chicken soup nicely. They also freeze well for later.

Heat on stove until just starting to boil (being careful not to burn, this is an important step in helping the buns rise nice and fluffy):
» 2 cups milk

Take off heat and pour into a large mixing bowl. Blend together with (Use kneading attachment if blending in electric mixer):
» 1 cup cool water
» ⅓ cup butter softened

Let sit to cool until still warm but no longer hot. Get rest of ingredients ready while you are waiting for it to come to a warm temperature. Mix together with milk mixture when ready:
» ¼ cup honey
» 2 large eggs (mix eggs together before adding to the mixture)

Blend dry ingredients together in a separate bowl. Then slowly add to the wet ingredients while kneading:
» 2 cups flour
» ¼ cup sugar
» ½ tsp salt
» 1½ tbsp. quick rise yeast

Slowly add in 5–6 more cups of flour (or as much flour is needed) while kneading, until dough is just sticky to the touch. Knead for an additional 4–5 minutes until dough is smooth to improve elasticity for a nice and fluffy rise.

When done kneading, rub a small amount of butter over top of the dough to keep towel from sticking. Cover with a clean hand towel (Make sure your dough is in a large enough bowl to rise to double in size).

Set aside to rise for about one hour or until doubled in size in your warm kitchen (or a warm oven if your kitchen is cold but don't leave your stove on if you do this!).

Knead down. Butter top again and cover. Set aside about one hour or doubled in size.

Knead down. If you are making cinnamon buns, now is the time to set aside one-quarter to one-half of the dough depending on how many cinnamon buns you want.

Form the rest of the dough into buns by squeezing out a small ball with your hand. Place ball onto buttered cookie sheet or in baking pan. Leave room between the buns for rising. Cover and let rise about 30–45 minutes, or until about doubled in size, then place into preheated 350°F oven.

Bake for about 10–15 minutes or until the tops are just starting to brown.

To make the cinnamon buns;

Roll out the dough you set aside with a rolling pin on a clean floured surface until about ¼-inch thick. Spread about a tablespoon of melted butter across the dough.

Sprinkle generous layer of brown sugar (about ¼–½ cup or so) just to cover the dough.

Sprinkle with cinnamon to taste. Optional: add in a sprinkle of raisins.

Drizzle about 1 tbsp. melted butter on the bottom of a baking pan. Add a thin sprinkle of brown sugar just to cover the bottom of the pan.

Roll up dough lengthwise and cut into about 1-inch thick rolls. Place each roll, cut side down into baking pan, leaving room between rolls for rising. Let rise until about doubled in size about half hour or so. Cook in preheated 350°F oven until just browned on top – about 15–20 minutes.

Creamy Greek Salad

We love Greek restaurants mainly because they make the best Greek salad dressing! This is my own Greek salad rendition. I love making this as a last-minute salad to throw together. Double the dressing and add in a cup or two of pasta or lettuce to make the salad go even further.

The Dressing

Mix together in medium sizes serving bowl:
- » 2 tbsp. mayonnaise
- » 2 tbsp. olive oil or avocado oil
- » 2 tbsp. red wine vinegar or apple cider vinegar (or even white vinegar is ok if that's all you have on hand)
- » ½ tsp honey
- » 1 tbsp. Greek seasoning mix
- » Dash of salt and pepper to taste

The Salad

Finely chop veggies and add all the following ingredients to the salad dressing:

- 1 cup peppers, any colour
- ½ cup Feta cheese
- ½ cup red onion
- 1 cup cherry tomatoes
- 1 cup cucumbers
- Optional: ½ cup olives

Warm potato salad

Who doesn't love a baked potato with all the fixings? This is the best of all of that. I add in a few veggies because well, maybe it makes it slightly healthier? The pressure cooker is a fast and yummy way to bake the potatoes.

Mix together in a medium sized serving bowl:
- » ½ cup mayonnaise
- » ½ cup sour cream (or plain Greek yogurt for a healthier version)
- » ½ cup chopped chives or green onions
- » ½ cup cheddar cheese grated (or a parmesan or mozzarella could work too. Get creative here for a more elevated flavour)
- » ½ cup bacon bits
- » 1 tsp lemon juice
- » 1 tsp relish
- » ½ tsp mustard
- » 1 tsp garlic spice mix (or ranch dressing)

» Salt and pepper to taste

Add to bowl:
» About 2 cups of potatoes, baked and cut into bite-sized cubes (nugget potatoes work great for this and don't even need peeling).

Optional add-ins:
» ½ cup finely chopped red peppers
» ½ cup cooked corn

Stir together and serve warm. Garnish with chopped parsley. Warm in microwave just before serving if you want to make this ahead of time. Double or triple recipe for a larger crowd. Serves about 4–5.

Meatloaf cupcakes

A rendition of mom's never fail meatloaf, this one is simple, and fun, made into individual cupcakes. Double or triple recipe as needed

Mix together in medium sized bowl:
- » 1lb ground beef
- » 1 egg
- » ½ cup smashed croutons
- » 1 clove finely chopped garlic
- » Sprinkle of salt and pepper
- » 1tbsp. Worcestershire sauce
- » ¼ cup Ketchup

Place beef mixture into muffin tins. Fill just to the top of each cup. Top with BBQ sauce.

Place in preheated 350°F oven about 15- 20 minutes or until fully cooked. Makes about 6-7 mini loaves.

These fun mini meatloaves are amazing, quick to cook, and great for lunches the next day. Serve with the Greek salad and the warm potato salad for dinner.

Let's not forget the dessert!

Individual Trifles

The ideas are endless with these yummy serving sized desserts. They taste even better if they are made the day ahead.

Choose your favourite glass cups such as cute little drinking glasses, small mason jars, or even wineglasses can work. Or layer in a large punch bowl to keep your assembly quick and simple.

Bake your favourite chocolate cake. While the chocolate cake is cooling, prep your whipped cream cheese icing, and make the caramel sauce. (Make this recipe even easier with store bought whipping cream and caramel sauce, but may not taste quite as amazing with premade ingredients)

1. Fill cup half full with chocolate cake
2. Layer with 2 tbsp. of cherry pie filling or raspberries
3. Add 1 tbsp. caramel sauce
4. Top with whipped cream cheese icing just to the top of the cup (put your icing into a large freezer storage bag and cut the tip off for a clean way to top your cups in icing)
5. Sprinkle over the top shaved chocolate, toffee bits, or a small piece of chocolate for garnish

Need a fresh summer option?

Keeping the same steps in mind, use the following ingredients:
1. Fill cup half full of Angel food cake or French vanilla cake
2. Add 2 tbsp. fresh berries or peaches
3. Layer to top of cup with whipped cream cheese icing
4. Top with a couple of fresh berries and a mint leaf for garnish
   Refrigerate a couple of hours before serving or even overnight for optimal flavours!

Dreamy Whipped Cream Icing

Make your whipping cream with whipped setting of your mixer. Whip together:
- 2 cup liquid whipping cream
- 1 cup icing sugar
- 2 tsp vanilla

Blend in until it just forms stiff peaks and is well mixed with whipping cream:
- 1½ cups cream cheese

Set aside in fridge until ready to assemble.

Best Caramel Sauce

A wonderful friend gave me this no fail caramel recipe. Use it to top other desserts but it pairs well in these yummy little trifle cups.

Melt over medium-high heat while stirring:
- 1 cup brown sugar
- ½ cup butter

Bring just to a light boil. When reaches light boil, boil for one more minute while stirring constantly. Take off heat and let sit 5 minutes. Stir in:
- 1 tsp vanilla
- 2 tbsp. cream or milk

May get foamy as you stir in:
- ½ tsp baking soda

And it's ready to serve. Store any leftovers in the fridge to heat up as needed.

Conclusion

home may be a lot to take in, but I suggest going through this book again and again, as you redesign your home. You can do this, my friend! Don't be afraid to make mistakes along the way. Mistakes are how we learn and grow. Sometimes as we clear away the clutter, we begin to see other areas that need work as well. This is the goal. One step at a time, we keep processing, growing, and moving forward in our homes … and our hearts. We are ever-changing. We will never arrive but hopefully we can find joy in the process, because if we are not growing, we are just going backwards.

Creating a peaceful home starts in your heart. When we are stuck in our hurts, fear, and anger, our homes can reflect the mess going on inside our own heads. Our experiences spill out into how we respond to our family members, and even can affect how cluttered our home gets, or our need for perfection and control. We all have a story. Dealing with our inner issues is important to respond to each other in love, creating a "safer" feeling home to thrive in and not just survive.

If only I could put into words, the incredible blessings the Lord has given me through surrendering my will to His. My story has not been wasted, not my mistakes, tears or pain. It has all been used for His greater purpose and plan for my life. The peace I experience through Christ is beyond all understanding. The joy and victory the Lord has brought in my life has been worth the fight to persevere. It's only in His presence I really see the beauty that surrounds us, even when life is well … a little chaotic. The Lord loves beauty. He is the author of beauty! I pray we can stop to enjoy the beauty He has blessed us with, so we can bless others in return.

Redesigning your home can help you enjoy the beauty of your home too. This may help you make decisions with any renovations you decide to do. Being able to see what needs to be addressed once the clutter is cleaned up will save you money from unnecessary updates.

Remember to create balance with your heights, furniture placement, accessories, and colours you use throughout your space. Use items that tell the story – your story. Your home should reflect who you are and what you love. Remember that a perfect space is not the goal but functional, peaceful, and cozy is. It's all about playing around with what you have until it sings to you. My clients laugh at me as I arrange, step back, rearrange again … and again … playing around with their accessories until it becomes pleasing to my eyes. It's fun! I didn't learn overnight either; it took time, much practice, and training, but keeping these tools in mind, will help you know how to redesign your space just as it did for me, and for the many wonderful clients I have worked with.

We all need a home to get creative, find rest, be silly, and experience joy together. Sometimes just a fresh design update is all we need to inspire us again. Or sometimes it's healing for our hearts that helps us find peace and enjoy those around us. Whatever the need is, I am so excited to have gotten to know you while sharing these simple redesign tools. Now go create a simple yummy dinner and enjoy your freshly updated space with your family and friends! My prayer is you find a new love and freedom to enjoy everyday life at home with the ones you love.

Maybe you will still hire a local designer and that's okay. You will go in being savvy and equipped to make even better design decisions with your professional. You are more than welcome to find me for more heart and home inspiration, or even catch my online design services at angelablock.com. Happy restoring your heart and your home my friend, because when your heart is restored… your home is restored too!

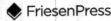 FriesenPress

Suite 300 - 990 Fort St
Victoria, BC, V8V 3K2
Canada

www.friesenpress.com

Photo credits go to:
Many of the photos in this book have been taken by me personally while working on some of my design projects. But many of these photos in this book are curtesy of these fabulous photographers;
- Khaptive design @khaptivedesign
- Belles and babies
- Ashley Block @a_dventure_
-jenniferaudreyphotography.com, @jenniferaudreyphoto
-The furniture and accessories in the inspiration board were provided and purchased from Urban Barn, Pier One imports, and Homesense stores.
-Adobe stock images

Recommended design resources:
-For more advice on designing with color and how to choose your undertones, check out www.mariakillam.com
-For more redesign training or to hire a redesigner/stager in your area, check out www.canadianredesignersassociation.org/

ISBN
978-1-5255-2886-6 (Hardcover)
978-1-5255-2887-3 (Paperback)
978-1-5255-2888-0 (eBook)

1. HOUSE & HOME, DECORATING

Distributed to the trade by The Ingram Book Company

FURNITURE LAYOUT

PAINT CHIPS

WALL COLOUR	TRIM COLOUR/ NEUTRAL #1
NEUTRAL #2	ACCENT COLOUR #1
ACCENT COLOUR #2	ACCENT COLOUR #3